Out of the saltshaker

Out of the saltshaker
Evangelism as a way of life

Rebecca Manley Pippert

Foreword by Walter Trobisch

Inter-Varsity Press

Inter-Varsity Press
38 De Montfort Street, Leicester LE1 7GP, England

First British edition 1980
Reprinted 1980, 1981, 1982

ISBN 0 85110 411 8

Printed in Great Britain by
Collins, Glasgow

*Inter-Varsity Press is the publishing division of the Universities and
Colleges Christian Fellowship (formerly the Inter-Varsity Fellowship), a
student movement linking Christian Unions in universities and colleges
throughout the British Isles, and a member movement of the International
Fellowship of Evangelical Students. For information about local and
national activities in Great Britain write to UCCF, 38 De Montfort
Street, Leicester LE1 7GP.*

*To Wes who is gentle, strong
and insatiably curious
about God's world*

Foreword

This is a book about the second turning.

In the first turning, a Christian experiences the transformation from a natural person to a spiritual person. Instead of "self" being the center of life—exploring, cultivating, adoring it—God becomes the center. This miracle is brought forth by the Holy Spirit giving us new life in Christ. It is a necessary, indispensable, basic step.

But it is only a first step. The work of the Holy Spirit should not stop here but lead to a second turning in which the spiritual person again becomes natural.

It is this second turning which enables Christians to communicate their faith. Not as a duty they must add to their many other Christian duties. Not as a program they have to adopt, a special technique they must learn. Not as a must at all, not as something they should do or may do or can do or will do.

The second turning makes the communication of faith—evangelism—something they are unable not to do. Something they cannot help but do. It flows out of Christians without their even realizing it. It arms them with contagious health. It becomes—to use Becky Pippert's word—*natural*. It becomes a way of life. To use a biblical term, it becomes *automatic*.

This term is used only once in the Bible. In Mark 4:28 Jesus tells the parable of the self-growing seed. To describe this process he uses the Greek word *automatos*.

Communication of faith thus becomes automatic, natural, something which happens even though the communicator—the sower—"knows not how" (Mk. 4:27). Something that goes on even while he sleeps or goes about his work. This is the result of the second turning—as indispensable as the first.

The second turning is what this book is all about.

I first met the author (who was then single) as a participant of a family life seminar in Oregon which I conducted with my wife, Ingrid. God has given Becky an outgoing, captivating personality.

I am haunted by this thought: what might have happened to her if she had never taken the first turning? Would she be using these gifts as a beautiful young woman for her own self-glory in a destructive way?

But I am even more haunted by the thought: what if she had stopped at the first turning? What if after becoming a Christian she had—out of a misunderstanding of the concept of holiness and spirituality—denied her natural beauty, her natural radiance, her natural gift of communication instead of using those gifts for the service of the Lord and becoming "natural" again?

Captivated by her Lord, her way of life became captivating. Disturbed by her Lord, her way of life became disturbing.

This is a dangerous book you are going to read. The same thing might happen to you. Evangelism might become your way of life.

Walter Trobisch

Preface

This book had its beginnings before I became a Christian. Even then I had definite thoughts about the way people communicated what was most important to them. I remember once encountering a zealous Christian. His brow was furrowed, he seemed anxious and impatient, and he sounded angry. Then he told me God loved me. I couldn't help notice the difference between his message and his style. His message was arresting (*me*—a sinner?) but ultimately appealing (a just and holy God who loves me deeply). But his style put me off. I recall thinking, "If God is so good and loving, then why is this guy so uptight?" Surely, the way we communicate a message of good news should be as marvelous as the message itself. This book is about getting our message and our style together.

Jesus tells us in the Sermon on the Mount that we are the salt of the earth. And he challenges us not to lose our savor— our saltiness. This means—among other things—that we are to be active in the world as his representatives. We are to get out of the saltshaker and into life itself. Not to be trodden down, but to be zestful witnesses to Jesus as Lord and Savior, as the one who alone gives life and meaning to a dying world.

I owe many people for their contribution to this book. My family gave me a joy and zest for life that were perhaps the greatest foundation I could have ever received for reaching out to others. They taught me how to celebrate.

It was Mrs. Ethel Renwick who first introduced me to Christ by reflecting both the love of God and the truth of the gospel. Her life illustrates what this book is all about.

My experiences as an undergraduate student in Spain were also critical to my growth and understanding of evangelism. There I met Ruth Siemens. She demonstrated Christ's love to me and to all of my friends whom I would drag over for a meal. But it was the way she lived that taught me more than anything else about lifestyle evangelism. I respect her profoundly.

My experiences in the Inter-Varsity Christian Fellowship chapter at the University of Illinois shaped me too. But most important have been my nearly seven years as a staff member with Inter-Varsity, both in the Pacific Northwest and presently in Washington, D.C. The teaching I have received from experienced Christians has been stimulating and substantial. I often bat around ideas with fellow staff. These have molded my life. I have especially appreciated the freedom to develop ideas and put them into practice. I have never had the slightest restraint put upon me because I am a woman. Rather I was constantly encouraged to use and develop my gifts. For this I owe great thanks to Fred Wagner and Jim Berney, as well as the Northwest staff team, all remarkable people. I have also been influenced by the teaching of Rev. Earl Palmer and inspired by the wisdom and lives of two very special people: Gene and Gerry Thomas.

My thanks go as well to several people for their help as I prepared this book. I bent several ears because of my fascination with, and unanswered questions about, the Pharisees.

Tom McAlpine was a real help as was Richard McClelland. Conversations with biblical scholars, Dr. Bernard Ramm and Dr. J. Barton Payne, were enlightening. I pulled all of this together in many hours of research and reflection at the Library of Congress, happily one block from my home. I want to thank Vicki Crawford who suggested the title as we dined over an Indonesian meal in Amsterdam. My newly wedded husband and I spent hours in highly animated discussion over the finer points of Judaic theology, modern evangelism and the art form of the written word. His help and skill and persistent love have been invaluable.

A note about other people whose names appear in the book is also in order. Except for Mary (in chapter one) and Stephanie (in chapter ten), the names of all of those whom I mention by only a first name have been changed to preserve their privacy.

The book itself springs from a deep-seated conviction: I believe that much of our evangelism is ineffective because we depend too much upon technique and strategy. Evangelism has slipped into the sales department. I am convinced that we must look at Jesus, and the quality of life he calls us to, as a model for what to believe and how to reach out to others. This basic assumption underlies both the content and the structure of this book.

The first six chapters look at Jesus' life, values and lifestyle with a view toward helping us be so Christlike in our own way of life that evangelism will come naturally. Chapters seven and eight focus on practicing the presence of Jesus. The final four chapters discuss the very practical issues of learning conversational skills and taking advantage of the good reasons God has given us for worshiping Jesus as Lord and Savior.

It is my hope that those who read this book will indeed be freed to live as salt and light, that they will be Christ's agents of healing in a broken world.

Uptight in Barcelona

1

CHRISTIANS AND NON-CHRISTIANS have something in common: We're both uptight about evangelism. Our fear as Christians seems to be, "How many people did I offend this week?" We think that we must be a little obnoxious in order to be good evangelists. A tension builds inside: Should I be sensitive to people and forget about evangelism, or should I blast them with the gospel and forget about their dignity as human beings? Many Christians choose to be aware of the person but then feel defensive and guilty for not evangelizing.

A Year Abroad

I certainly felt that way during my junior year abroad at the University of Barcelona, Spain. Of course, I wanted my friends to know God. But every time I got up courage to be vocal about Jesus, an image leaped into my mind of an ag-

gressive Christian buttonholing an unwitting victim. As a
nonbeliever I had thought many Christians were weird,
spreading leaflets on street corners and nabbing strangers. I
was terrified that if I said anything at all about Christ, my
friends would consider me just as strange. And I would agree
with them. There was a part of me that secretly felt evangelism
was something you shouldn't do to your dog, let alone a
friend.

To evangelize, it seemed, required insensitivity and an
inclination to blurt out a memorized gospel outline, without
inhaling, to every stranger you met. It never occurred to me
that my pre-Christian, unredeemed, almost common-sense
understanding about how to relate warmly to people might be
valid. For instance, I knew how offended I had been as a non-
Christian when someone tried to push religion on me, without
even discovering who I was or what I believed. That was a
proper response, I see now, for I should be offended when
I'm being treated as someone's evangelistic project instead of
as a person.

Yet when I became a Christian I thought I was supposed to
toss in my common-sense perceptions in order to be spiritual.
I thought I was called to "offend for Jesus' sake!" How I
thought I was supposed to evangelize went against my very
grain. But, I felt, with a somewhat twisted logic, "Is it really so
much to ask that I turn people off as soon as I meet them,
when you think of all that Christ has done for me?"

Still, I knew Christians were called on to do hard things.
And because it was so hard to do I thought such evangelism
had to be spiritual. The result was that I would put off
witnessing as long as possible. Whenever the guilt became too
great to bear, I overpowered the nearest non-Christian with a
nonstop running monolog and then dashed away thinking,
"Whew! Well, I did it. It's spring of '74 and hopefully the guilt
won't overcome me again till winter of '75." (And my non-
Christian friends hoped the same!)

I witnessed like a Pavlovian dog. The bell would ring, I would get ready, activated, juices running and then BAM! I'd spit it out.

Paradoxically I also knew that unless I really cared for my skeptic friends, they would never be interested in the gospel. I was deeply moved by the way Jesus demonstrated compassion to the people he met. I wanted to do the same, although it didn't occur to me that this had much to do with evangelism. So I tried to reach out and care for the people God had placed around me. But I felt guilty for not giving a gospel outline to every nonbeliever I met.

It wasn't that I never spoke about my faith; in retrospect, however, I was far too paranoid about people's responses to me and consequently too silent. But one thing hindered me from speaking: I felt that unless I gave a person the whole ball of wax, all at one time, then I wasn't "evangelizing." So when my friends at the University of Barcelona said they were curious about my faith and began asking questions, I thought, "Isn't that *amazing*! And I wasn't even evangelizing!"

And so I approached my year abroad in Spain, seeking to establish caring relationships with students and asking God to touch their lives. I also asked him to teach me how to evangelize and to free me from fear.

During this time I lived with Ruth Siemens, a staff worker in Spain and Portugal for the International Fellowship of Evangelical Students. She is a remarkable woman, abounding in gifts, intelligence, zest and vision. Every time we talked about my desire for ministry she suggested I start a Bible study for my non-Christian friends. I acted as though it was an interesting idea. But to myself I thought, "Well, that's what happens when you've been on the mission field too long. You sort of lose touch with reality."

But Ruth was persistent, and at last I decided to do it even though I thought it was ridiculous. She helped by coaching me on what to say as I asked my friends to a study on the life of

Christ. Assuming I was having a conversation that related to spiritual things, I could say, "How would you like to come to a study on the biographies of Jesus Christ?" or, "Wouldn't it be fascinating to examine primary source documents to see for ourselves what Jesus has to say and who he claims to be?"

When the actual moment arrived, my fear was so great that it reduced me to a rather catatonic state, and I mumbled, "You don't want to come to a Bible study, do you?" To my amazement and alarm they all thought it was a great idea and were eager to come. The study was to begin the following Wednesday evening at my apartment.

One of the surprises was the kind of people who wanted to come. Without realizing it, I had formed a mental picture of the people that God would lead me to. I expected it to be the "likely" looking ones: those who seemed a bit passive or lonely or vulnerable. But it wasn't at all the anemic types that God brought into my life. They all seemed terribly normal. They were vital, opinionated, interesting people who had strong questions about the existence of God as well as about everything else. They were stimulating to be around, but I would never have thought of them as being open to spiritual things.

Then I met Mary. She was an Irish girl taking a year's study in Spain. She was bright, funny and had a ready quip for everything. I invited her over for a meal to meet my roommates. I wondered if she would be interested in coming to the Bible study. Suddenly, not knowing yet that I was a Christian, she said, "This has been the best month I've had all year! Do you know that I've talked three people out of being Christians this month!"

I gulped and thought, "Thank goodness I didn't ask her to the Bible study! I would die if someone like that ever came."

The next day I ran into her after class and she smirked, "See you next Wednesday at seven. What a lark *that* would be! I wouldn't miss it for the world!"

I smiled blankly and said it would be great, but nothing registered in my mind. What was I doing next Wednesday? *Wednesday!* Oh, no—it wasn't possible. How did she find out? Who told her? Nothing could possibly be worse than Mary coming.

I raced to my apartment to tell Ruth and my other roommate, Kathy Lang, the terrible news. Then I noticed a sly expression on their faces. "OK," I demanded, "which one of you did it? Who betrayed me?"

They laughed but refused to confess. They said simply that God was answering my prayer by bringing spiritually open students to the Bible study. I moaned and wondered who else God would bring that would be as open and receptive as Mary. One thing was clear. God and I had drastically different opinions about who was spiritually open. He seemed to have a special attraction to hard-core cases. And I felt he wanted to give them all to me.

I had Christians all over Barcelona praying. It was almost my first experience in leading a Bible study and to do it with a group mostly of nonbelievers terrified me. Then Wednesday came. The study was to begin at 7:00. It was 7:15 when the doorbell finally rang. I opened the door, expecting to see the crowd, but there stood Mary, alone. She sauntered in, took a quick look around and said, "My, looks like you're really packing them in tonight."

"Ah, well, you know how busy everyone is, and it's early yet. Listen, make yourself at home and I'll be right back," I said as I dashed to the bathroom, closed the door and burst into tears. I felt so ridiculous. Everyone was praying for me and would ask how the Bible study went. And then of all people to show up it had to be Mary.

I returned and decided to make polite conversation, thinking she would leave soon. Instead she abruptly asked, "Why are you a Christian? How can you be a thinking person and reject your mind? It's intellectual suicide to believe something without any evidence to support it."

"Mary," I said with unexpected courage, "I couldn't agree with you more. I've always been amazed by people who can accept Christ blindly. But you know what else mystifies me? How anyone can *reject* Christianity blindly without bothering to investigate the evidence." And so began a two-hour conversation. We discussed such issues as the historicity of the New Testament documents, the uniqueness of Jesus and the evidence for the resurrection. It seemed largely an intellectual exercise to me.

Then as she was leaving I popped John Stott's book *Basic Christianity* into her hands. "Read it sometime in the next couple of years," I said as she walked out the door. No one could have ever accused me of using pressure tactics.

The next day the others who were supposed to come to the study apologized and said they had completely forgotten. But they promised they would be there next Wednesday. And next Wednesday came. I felt reassured. God wouldn't let me go through another experience like that again. And once more I asked several Christians in Barcelona to pray.

So 7:00 came. Then 7:10, 7:15, 7:20 and finally the doorbell rang. I rushed to the door, eager to see my friends. I threw open the door, but only one person was standing there —Mary.

Once more she took a quick look around and said, "This Bible study is really dynamite, isn't it? Never seen such crowds."

That did it. This was the closest thing to martyrdom I'd ever experienced. "Mary, would you excuse me for a minute. I'll be right back," I said and rushed into the bathroom again. I couldn't believe it. This was the second week I had prepared the same passage. I had prayed every day. And the only "faithful" member was Mary!

I didn't understand, but I returned to Mary, hoping she would leave quickly so I could cry later. Instead she said, "I read that book you gave me. I came to that chapter on sin and I wanted to hide under the bed."

It never occurred to me as she spoke that the Holy Spirit was convicting her of sin. I merely thought it was a strange but interesting response. She plied me with questions and told me a great deal about her life and her family. I began to glimpse for the first time who she was—a sensitive young woman who covered her questions and wounds effectively. I was moved as she shared her life and I genuinely cared for her.

Still, her initial disdain and negativity toward Christianity intimidated me. I thought perhaps that God was seeking her. What I didn't see was that her badgering me with questions, her coming to the study, even her hostility and anger were real signs that she was grappling with God.

Then came the bomb. She suddenly looked straight at me and said, "I feel like God is over there," as she gestured with her hand, "and I am over here. I've really wanted to know God all of my life. But how do I bridge the gap? What would I do if I wanted to become a Christian?"

I stared at her in disbelief. No one had ever asked me that question. I not only felt inept, but terrified that at this crucial moment God wouldn't come through. I had wondered what I would do if this ever happened. But the same scenario had always plagued me. The person would ask me to become a Christian. I would say, "Fine. Let's just pray together and ask God to come into your life." We would pray and then she would say, "Ah, Becky, I hate to say this. But ... um ... I don't feel any different. I mean I feel just exactly the way I did before we prayed." I would secretly think, "Oh, *how* embarrassing!" But I would say, "Well, listen. Why don't we just try it again." We would pray again, but then she would tell me she still felt the same. Then I would say, "Well, look, it's Saturday. Maybe weekends are a busy time. Let's try it again next week." And I would escape as fast as I could. Just the thought of facing such an episode made me quake. And here was Mary, asking me to help her, immediately, directly and *now.*

"Well, what should I do?" Mary asked me.

"Ahhhh, well, I guess you could, um, pray," I answered weakly.

"I don't know how. What should I say?" she persisted.

"Well, ah, you could tell God what you told me," I stammered.

"Okay. *When* should I tell him?" she asked.

For the first time I brightened.

"You can tell him the *minute* you get home," I replied, leaping from my chair and ushering her quickly out of the room. "As soon as you get home just tell him everything," I said as I pushed her through the front door. "And read the last chapter of Stott's book on how to become a Christian," I shouted as she walked down the steps looking a bit bewildered.

I felt miserable. God wasn't asking John Stott to lead Mary to faith. He was asking me. And I felt I had failed. I had been ashamed and embarrassed. I felt inadequate and unqualified to help Mary. But most of all, I lacked the faith and the guts to believe God actually would come through and that he could use me. So I tried to forget the entire incident. After all, maybe Mary had just had a bad day. She was probably feeling emotional and would have been terribly embarrassed later if I had done anything anyway.

The next day Ruth returned from a trip. As I recounted my experience with Mary to her, she became more and more excited. Before I could even finish she interrupted, her eyes shining, and she said, "Oh, Becky, then you led her to Christ, right?"

And I answered, a bit subdued, "No, actually, I led her out the door."

It was the only time I ever saw Ruth unable to cover her disappointment. "Becky! Why not? You've led other friends to Christ, haven't you?"

"Ah, well, let's see now. It's kind of hard to remember. I guess, ah, *actually*—ah . . . no."

Mary returned to my apartment a few days later. I was amazed to hear her account of what happened after she left me and amused by how she described it. She told Ruth in a somewhat exasperated tone, "Well, I asked Becky what to do and she told me to go home. But at least she said to read the last chapter of that book. Now listen, I really do believe this stuff and I prayed that prayer at the end of the book. Does that mean I'm 'in'?"

Ruth assured her that she was indeed a child of God. But I remained somewhat skeptical and waited to see the results. The results, by the way, were that Mary grew steadily and is a Christian to this day. I need also to say that since that experience nearly ten years ago, I have rarely seen someone convert to Christ as quickly as she did. God had been working on her a long time before I ever met her. But seemingly quick conversions are the exception, in my experience, not the norm.

Being Yourself

Two feelings came from this experience. One was a feeling of failure. I think we could safely say, by most standards, that I failed. I felt sadness over my lack of faith and courage—but not despair. In fact, my other feeling was hope. That experience made me realize that when God is seeking a person, he will not allow my fear, my feeling of intimidation or my lack of knowledge or experience to prevent that person from finding him. With all the mistakes I still had seen the power of God at work overcoming my clumsiness and helping me to speak to Mary.

The more I reflected, the more I realized that I couldn't have done it worse. And yet, Mary had survived me! Even with all my mistakes, God had used me. Granted I wasn't much more than a warm body sitting in front of her. But I had guided her to the right book. At least I had *tried* to answer her questions, and I genuinely cared for her.

This experience forced me to reflect seriously about my problems in evangelism. I had thought that only with a slick presentation, a polished formula and memorized verses could anyone be successful in evangelism. But I discovered that God was indeed glorified in my weakness. If anyone had told me then that I would eventually be writing a book on evangelism, I would have laughed uproariously. The incongruity simply would have been too great. It has been a long pilgrimage, with many failures, from my experience with Mary to my work with students today. And even now when speaking to college students, I sense they are breathlessly waiting for the same thing that I was: a new argumentproof, jelled approach, the magic formula that works on one and all or your money back. But even if I had such a formula to sell, it still wouldn't work.

Our problem in evangelism is not that we don't have enough information—it is that we don't know how to be ourselves. We forget we are called to be witnesses to what we have seen and know, not to what we don't know. The key is authenticity and obedience, not a doctorate in theology. We haven't grasped that it really is okay for us to be who we are, when we are with non-Christians, even if we don't have all the answers to their questions or if our knowledge of Scripture is limited.

But there is a deeper problem here. Our uneasiness with non-Christians reflects our uneasiness with our own humanity. Because we are not certain about what it means to be human (or spiritual, for that matter), we struggle in relating naturally, humanly, to the world. For example, many of us avoid evangelism for fear that we will offend someone. Yet how often have we told a non-Christian that that's why we are hesitating?

At the University of California, Berkeley campus, I met a co-ed one afternoon in Sproul Plaza. Our conversation moved to whether we believed in God. It was an easy, almost casual talk. I began telling her about Jesus and she seemed interested. But as I became more enthusiastic about what it meant to be a Christian, she seemed to withdraw emotionally. Still I kept on talking about Jesus—for want of knowing what else to do. But even though my mouth kept moving, I was very aware that I was turning her off. So there I was, having a private conversation with myself, trying to figure out how to stop, while I could hear myself talking to her about Christ.

Suddenly I realized how ridiculous all this was, so I said, "Look, I feel really bad. I *am* very excited about who God is and what he's done in my life. But I hate it when people push 'religion' on me. So if I'm coming on too strong will you just tell me?"

She looked at me in disbelief. "I can't believe you just said that. I mean, I cannot *believe* you honestly said that," she answered.

"Why?" I asked.

"Well, I never knew Christians were aware that we hate being recipients of a running monolog," she answered. (So much for my evangelistic skill.)

"Listen," I responded, "most Christians I know are very hesitant to share their faith *precisely* because they're afraid they'll offend."

"But as long as you let people know that you're aware of where they're coming from, you can say anything you want!" she responded immediately. "And you just tell Christians that I said so."

Her response was perceptive. What she was saying was that when I told her that I hated to be someone's evangelistic project, I was also establishing that we had a great deal in common: I didn't want to dump the gospel and she didn't want to be dumped on. That is a natural response, a *human* response and a *shared* response. What surprised her was that I was human, too, not some superdisciple whose feet never touch the

ground. But I am offended by similar tactics. So on the basis of
our strong, common human bond, I was freed to communicate my faith.

God has given me increasing freedom to talk about him to
others. My experience with Mary made me realize that,
although some of my non-Christian friends had become open
to God through my influence, no one had ever become a
Christian in my presence. Even if they wanted to, I wouldn't
let them! As I pondered my discomfort about evangelism, I
discovered several things about myself.

For one thing, I was so afraid of being identified as a religious weirdo or a Jesus freak that I often remained silent when
the topic of God came up. How people saw me mattered more
than how God saw me. Ironically, most people respect and
respond to a person who has definite ideas and who com-
municates them clearly rather than to someone who seems
apologetic and wishy-washy. My experience in Spain con-
firmed that. I was amazed to see how "evangelistic" and bold
the Marxists on campus were. Their style wasn't obnoxious,
but they were convinced and it showed. They communicated
their beliefs articulately and with zeal. As I watched students
respond to them, I was surprised to see how open they were
and how much respect they had for someone who really
believed in something and was willing to stand up for it.

All of my paranoia about how I *thought* people would respond if I were bold about Christ had made me defensive. If I
had gone to a religious retreat, I would stammer when asked,
"How was your weekend?" Or I would tend to hide my Bible
under other books so my agnostic roommates wouldn't think I
was strange. (As if *that* kind of behavior would keep people
from thinking I was strange!)

I was behaving this way, I told myself, in order to be sensitive to non-Christians. But to them I looked weird and the
Marxists made sense. I finally had to agree with St. Paul that if
we fear God first, then we will try to persuade people (2 Cor.

5:11). Whatever you fear (or supremely respect) the most you will serve. Fearing what people thought of me, I served them and it backfired. When I began to fear and respect God the most and then serve him, I felt a new freedom to share my faith, whether I won a popularity contest or not. I didn't feel called to be offensive, just more bold. And the irony was that, since I wasn't trying to please them first but God, people listened and wanted to know more.

I found out something else. I didn't understand other people's genuine desire. Although I saw the needs and emptiness in the lives of my non-Christian friends, I couldn't imagine that it was Jesus Christ they were really searching for. Jesus was for "religious folk," not for my pagan friends. So because I never really expected them to respond to the gospel, they didn't.

This whole feeling was associated with my own self-doubt. I feared that Jesus was just "my trip." Wasn't it arrogant to suggest that my view was the only way? But as I grew to understand the nature of Christianity, I saw that our faith stands on historical data as well as subjective experience. Truth was the ultimate issue, not a feeling in my heart. God was not asking me to stand on my own ideas or emotions, but rather on the person and work of Jesus Christ. If anyone was guilty of being offensive, it was Jesus—not me. It was *his* idea that he was the only way to God, not mine. Realizing this freed me from cowering when accused of being narrow. I could answer, "I know, and isn't it amazing that Jesus actually said so many narrow things? Wouldn't it be intriguing to study him to discover why he made such egotistical claims?"

Still, I was paralyzed by the fear of offending people and forever ruining their chance of entering the kingdom. So I thought, "I'll just be nice and smile and hope they catch on." Well, Girl Scouts smile too, so that can't be all there is to witnessing for Christ. Furthermore, I realized that I was giving myself too much credit. What I was saying was that if I made one mistake or couldn't answer one of their questions, then it was all over. They were doomed. Their entire eternal destiny rested on my ability to know every answer. God might be eternal and powerful, but he could never again reach the person I had offended or the one whose question I could not answer.

It's odd. Offending people is rarely the problem. If you are sensitive enough to realize this can be a pitfall, then it is usually not your problem. What I often see on campuses is this: sensitive students who run around saying, "I'm just so afraid of being insensitive." So they remain silent when what they need to be is more bold. And, second, I hear students say proudly what they don't do. "I never have turned off anyone, like those other guys have." "I've never used any gimmicks or surveys or tracts, like those other guys." "I've never gone door knocking." It is easy for us to agree about what we don't do. But how thrilled will God be when he asks us what we have done with our lives, and we reel off everything we *didn't* do?

Finally, I saw that I had a problem with God. I couldn't talk about him in a natural way. I was fine until the topic of religion came up. Suddenly I felt as if I needed to sound spiritual, and instead of listening, I would panic because I couldn't remember any Scripture verses. My hands would get clammy; my eyes would dart from side to side in the hope that no one else was listening; the tone of my voice would change and I would begin talking "religiously." Then I would wonder why they always looked so uncomfortable when we talked about spiritual things. My problem was that I didn't think God could be a natural, integrated part of an ongoing discussion about movies, classes, exams or boyfriends. I didn't have an integrated Christian world view; God was compartmentalized and separated from "normal" living.

The Strength of Weakness
These new insights began to free me. As Mary grew and

flourished as a young Christian, it affected my faith and my ability to witness. But it was the conversion of another atheist friend of mine eight months later that brought fresh discoveries and permanent change into my life. I will tell that story later in chapter ten. But it was what Stephanie told me the night she became a Christian that startled me.

"At first I thought, fine, let Becky have her religion—that's her bag," she said. "I'm not the least bit interested, but if that's her thing then it's all right with me. Then you invited me to dinner and before we ate you asked if we could thank God for the food. I thought, 'Oh, how quaint.' Only you didn't just thank him for the food—you thanked him for *me* and our friendship! It made me feel so good inside. I never thought you felt our relationship had anything to do with God. But then I thought, 'That's ridiculous—thanking someone who doesn't exist for me.'

"Then we went to the Bergman film and afterward you said you'd studied the very same concept that was in the film in the Bible that day. I never dreamed God would have anything remotely in common with modern cinema! Another day you invited me to an objective, no-strings-attached study of the person of Jesus in the Bible. Fine. Only the trouble was—I really liked the guy! He seemed so real as we would read about him each week.

"But you know what affected me most? All my life I used to think, 'How arrogant for someone to call himself a Christian, to think he's that good.' But then I got to know you—and Becky, you are far from perfect, yet you call yourself a Christian. So my first shock was to discover <u>you 'blow it' like I do</u>. <u>But the biggest shock was that y</u><u>ou admitted it, where I</u> <u>couldn't</u>. Suddenly I saw that being a Christian didn't mean never failing, but admitting when you've failed. I wanted to keep Christ in a box and let you be religious during Bible studies. But the more you let me inside your life, the more impossible it became to keep the lid on Christianity. Even your admission of weaknesses drove me to him!"

That confession changed my life. What astonished me was that she had seen me in all kinds of circumstances—she had seen the real me—and it gave the gospel more power, not less. I had always thought I should cover up my doubts and problems, because if she knew me she wouldn't become a Christian. But the more open and transparent I was (even with my weaknesses), the more real Jesus Christ became to her.

Please get this straight. In saying we must be human with each other, I am not condoning sin. God calls us to perfection. I am not suggesting we share our weaknesses as if we were in a "competitive sinning" match in order to be real. Sin isn't God's brand of humanity: perfect obedience is. But so is humble confession when we fail. So our goal must be to live within the balance of aiming for perfect obedience and complete openness. The paradox I constantly experience is that as I allow people inside—to see who I am with the pain and problems as well as the successes—they tell me they see God. It's when I cover up (ironically, for "God's reputation") and try to appear "together," with no problems, that they can see only Becky.

I had to learn from experience what Scripture teaches in 1 Thessalonians 2:8: to share the gospel we must share our life, our very selves. If we don't grasp that Christ has freed us to be authentic, we will see evangelism as a project instead of a lifestyle. And we will tend to see non-Christians more as objects of our evangelistic efforts than as authentic persons.

I once asked a girl if she felt comfortable about evangelism "Oh, yes!" she responded. "I do it twice a week." (Somehow it sounded more like taking multiple vitamins.) Evangelism isn't just something you "do"—out there—and then get back to normal living. Evangelism involves taking people seriously, getting across to their island of concerns and needs, and then sharing Christ as Lord in the context of our natural living situations.

The problem stems from our great difficulty in believing

that <u>God is glorified in our utter humanity,</u> rather than in our spiritually programmed responses. Most of us fear that who we are inside just isn't enough. So we cover up our honest questions and doubts thinking we won't sound spiritual. But in doing this we forfeit our most important asset in evangelism—our real person. Not to accept our humanness means we lose our point of authentic contact with the world. We, of all people, should be offering the world a picture of what it means to be truly human. Yet it is often Christians who fear their humanity more than anyone else. When we get a good look at Jesus we will see that it is not our humanity we need to fear.

Jesus the Evangelist

2

OUR HUMANITY IS NOT OUR problem in evangelism. The most human of all human beings had no difficulty with who he was. Jesus came to us as the first whole person since Adam and Eve before the Fall. It is Jesus, then, who provides for us the model of what it means to be human. By following his lead we will not only become more like God himself but we will find ourselves becoming more comfortable with our humanity and with evangelism which will begin to flow naturally from who we are.

Jesus, One of Us

Jesus told us that as the Father sent him into the world, so he is sending us (Jn. 17:18). How then did the Father send him? Essentially he became one of us. The Word became flesh (Jn. 1:14). God didn't send a telegram or shower evangelistic Bible study books from heaven or drop a million bumper stickers from the sky saying, "Smile, Jesus loves you." He sent a man, his Son, to communicate the message. His strategy hasn't changed. He still sends men and women—before he sends tracts and techniques—to change the world. You may think this strategy is risky, but that is God's problem, not yours.

In Jesus, then, we have our model for how to relate to the world, and it is a model of openness and identification. Jesus was a remarkably open man. He didn't think it was unspiritual for him (fully realizing he was the Son of God) to share his physical needs (Jn. 4:7). He didn't fear losing his testimony by revealing to his disciples the depths of his emotional stress in the Garden of Gethsemane (Mk. 14:32-52). Here is our model for genuine godliness. We see him asking for support and desiring others to minister to him. We must learn then to relate transparently and genuinely to others because that is God's style of relating to us. Jesus commands us to go and then preach, not to preach and then leave. We are not to shout the gospel from a safe and respectable distance, and remain detached. We must open our lives enough to let people see that we too laugh and hurt and cry. If Jesus left all of heaven and glory to become one of us, shouldn't we at least be willing to leave our dorm room or Bible study circle to reach out to a friend?

There is also confusion about what it means to be spiritual. We feel it is more spiritual to take our non-Christian roommate to a Bible study or to church than to a play or out for pizza. Just as we do not understand our natural points of contact with the world: we don't understand our natural points of contact with God himself. He made us human. He is therefore interested in every aspect of our humanness. We dare not limit him to Bible studies and discussions with Christians. He created life and he desires to be glorified in the totality of all that adds up to life. And his power and presence will come crashing through to the world as we let him live fully in every aspect of our lives.

How can we relate to people in a way that will change the

world? Jesus did it in two ways: by his radical identification with men and women, and by his radical difference. Jesus seemed to respond to people by noticing first what they had in common (Jn. 4:7). But it was often in the context of their similarities that Jesus' difference came crashing through (Jn. 4:10).

As people discovered Jesus' profound humanness, they began to recognize his deity. God's holiness became shattering and penetrating as Jesus confronted people on their very own level of humanity. But the point is that it took both, his radical identification and his radical difference, to change the world. So it will be for us.

Jesus the Delightful

I reread the Gospels a year ago out of a desire to "rediscover Jesus." I was a bit alarmed by several attitudes that I sensed increasingly among students. One was that the Gospels were light reading for the spiritually young whereas the Epistles were the real meat and potatoes for the mature. Another was an attitude that focused *only* on the Gospels but manipulated Jesus into being the Lord of their particular cause.

If a disciple must first master the life of the Master, then we need to grapple in radical, accurate and penetrating ways with the Gospels as they reveal the person of Jesus. As I read again, Jesus struck me with fresh force.

My first impression was that Jesus was utterly delightful. He enjoyed people. He liked to go to parties and to weddings. He was the kind of man people invited for dinner. And he came. He went to where they were. When two men first approached him, they became tongue-tied and unsure of what to say (Jn. 1:35-39). When Jesus asked them what they wanted, they responded, "Oh, well . . . we were kind of wondering where your apartment is." Now Jesus knew that how he decorated his apartment was not the burning issue in their hearts. But instead of delivering a sermon, he took them *home*

with him, and they became his disciples. Later some of their
relatives were among the first people he healed. But Jesus was
more than merely charming; he cared about building a sense
of family.

Jesus established intimacy with people quickly. Partly it was
because he was open, but also because he understood people
and wanted to establish rapport. He let people know that he
had a sense of who they were and that he appreciated them.
The first thing he did on meeting Simon was to give him a
nickname. The first thing he told Nathaniel was that he
recognized the basic honesty of his character. Jesus drew
people. Some came because Jesus recognized who they were,
others because they had glimpsed something of who he was.
He was approachable, he wanted people to know it, and they
did.

Children loved him. Adults were affected so much by him
that some just wanted to touch his clothes. Why? They saw
that Jesus loved them. His love was extravagant, almost
reckless—never cautious or timid. And he talked of his
Father's endless love.

The people of Jesus' day thought holy men were unap-
proachable. But Jesus' work was in the marketplace. He made
people feel welcome, and that they had a place. His life was a
constant demonstration that there were only two things that
really mattered in this life—God and people. They were the
only things that lasted forever.

Jesus was a compassionate man. He cared deeply and was
not afraid to show it. He was profoundly committed to setting
people free and making them whole. He touched people at
the deepest level. He wanted to heal not only blindness and
leprosy, but the things that prevented joy and beauty, and
freedom and justice.

The Stoics may have been proud of concealing their tears,
but he never concealed his. He showed them plainly on his
open face, whether he was weeping for a city or for a friend's

loss. He healed people because he cared about them, not merely so they would follow him. He saw a woman weeping over the loss of her only son (Lk. 7:11-17). No one asked him to do anything, probably feeling it was hopeless anyway. Moved with compassion, he took the initiative and brought the boy back to life. In fact, he even touched the bier on which the boy lay. As it was the Jewish practice to use the open bier, Jesus' touching it meant pollution according to ceremonial laws. But Jesus responded to human need first.

Once when Jesus was on his way to heal Jairus's daughter who was on the point of death, a woman who had been hemorrhaging for twelve years and had "suffered much under many physicians" suddenly touched his garment and was healed. Jesus had so much concern for her that he stopped long enough to find out who he had healed and to learn of her story. Can you imagine Jairus's anxiety as the long story unfolded? But Jesus listened patiently and lovingly.

On another occasion a leper came to Jesus, no doubt full of shame and wounds (Mk. 1:40-45). Timid but desperate he said, "Well, if you want to, I think you could heal me." And Jesus, moved with compassion and looking at him steadily said, "Oh, I want to," and healed him.

I was also struck by the practical dimension of Jesus' compassion. His feelings were no deeper than his practical concern. He healed Jairus's daughter, and at the moment of a stupendous miracle, he simply told them to get her something to eat. His care was consistent. Never flashy, sometimes almost quiet. Even after his death, Jesus demonstrated the very same care. If I had resurrected, I would have rented the Colliseum and staged the Mormon Tabernacle Choir to sing the "Hallelujah Chorus." But in one postresurrection account we find Jesus making the disciples a little breakfast!

Jesus was perceptive. He had an extraordinary ability to see beneath the myriad of layers of people and know what they longed for, or really believed, but were afraid of revealing. That is why his answers so frequently did not correspond to the questions he was asked. He sensed their unspoken need or question and responded to that instead. Jesus could have healed lepers in countless ways. To the leper in Mark 1:40-45 he could have shouted, "Be healed . . . but don't get too close. I just hate the sight of lepers." He did not. Jesus reached over and touched him. Jesus' touch was not necessary for his physical healing. It was critical for his emotional healing.

Can you imagine what it meant to that man to be touched? A leper was an outcast, quite accustomed to walking down a street and seeing people scatter, shrieking at him, "Unclean—unclean!" Jesus knew that this man not only had a diseased body but an equally diseased self-concept. He needed to be touched to be fully cured. And so Jesus responded as he always did, with total healing for the whole person.

If someone had asked me as an agnostic several years ago to describe what I thought Jesus was like, I would have readily given an answer. I pictured him as a sweet, kind man, his hair parted down the middle with a kind of Halo shampoo effect. I thought he probably spent most of his time skipping along the shores of Galilee, humming religious tunes with his disciples—the kind of person everyone would love, but especially your mother. I sincerely believed this and did not think it was the least irreverent. Granted, the depth of my biblical understanding stemmed largely from Cecil B. De Mille—and Hollywood seems to have a knack for making spirituality and severe anemia almost synonymous. But even from the few Christians I knew, I sensed that Jesus was something of a limp-wrist and several of them certainly behaved that way.

Then one day I looked at the New Testament. Instead of a meek, mild Jesus, I found a man of profound passion. An extraordinary being, flinging furniture down the front steps of the temple, casting out demons, and asking people how they expected to escape the damnation of hell. He said such bland, innocuous things as, "I came to cast fire on the earth"

Convincing/strong.

(Lk. 12:49). G. K. Chesterton points out that even his literary style reflects his passion. He writes, "The diction used *about* Christ has been, and perhaps wisely, sweet and submissive. But the diction used by Christ is quite curiously gigantesque; it is full of camels leaping through needles and mountains hurled into the sea." Moreover, his style consists of "an almost furious use of the 'a fortiori.' His 'how much more' is piled one upon another like castle upon castle in the clouds."[1] After seeing this shattering personality which fills the Gospels, having gotten even a glimpse of him, I could never, never again say with casual indifference, "Oh, how interesting."

Jesus the Exasperating

If my first impression of Jesus was that he was delightful, another equally forceful impression was that he was exasperating. Wherever he went he produced a crisis. He compelled individuals to decide, to make a choice. In fact he struck me as the most crisis-producing individual I had ever encountered. Eventually nearly everyone clashed with Jesus, whether they loved him or hated him.

A friend of mine has said that he always discovered a lot about a person when he knew who liked the person and who did not. In Jesus' case, we have the story of the holiest man who ever lived, and yet it was the prostitutes and lepers and thieves who adored him, and the religious who hated his guts.

Why did he cause so much controversy? I will examine this more closely in later chapters. But partly it was his unabashed claims. In his address at the synagogue, Luke tells us that he read from Isaiah, then as they looked straight at him he said, "Today this scripture has been fulfilled in your hearing" (Lk. 4:21). In other words, "It's become true *now* because it is fulfilled through *me*. You are looking at the fulfillment."

Characteristically, the first response was favorable as they "wondered" at his "gracious words." But on reflection they began to think, "Wait a minute, isn't this Joseph's boy?" Then Jesus mentioned that prophets have always been rejected by the people. And within moments they became so outraged they tried to kill him. They struggled not only with who Jesus said he was, but with who he said they were as well. He made them confront both themselves and him.

Other people were offended with Jesus because he violated their understanding of religion and piety. The religious of his day were particularly incensed that he deliberately healed on the Sabbath. But what do you do with a man who is supposed to be the holiest man who has ever lived and yet goes around talking with prostitutes and hugging lepers? What do you do with a man who not only <u>mingles with the most unsavory people but actually seems to enjoy them</u>? The religious accused him of being a drunkard, a glutton and having tacky taste in friends. As Gene Thomas is fond of saying, "Jesus was simply not your ideal Rotarian." It is a profound irony that the Son of God visited this planet and one of the chief complaints against him was that he was not religious enough.

The religious of his day were offended because he did not follow their rules and traditions. He was bold and outspoken. He favored extreme change and valued what they felt was insignificant, which was largely the "unlovely." Jesus knew the power and prestige of the Pharisees. And he knew they expected people to show deference to them. But he loved the Pharisees and wanted them to see plainly who they were and how far many of them were from God's kingdom.

What did he say to them? Well, I think Jesus would have been my *last* choice as a speaker for a fund-raising drive. To say he was not the master of subtlety would be putting it mildly. Imagine a scene in which you would gather all the powerful leaders and religious elite so they could hear Jesus give a talk. (Matthew 23 describes such a scene.) When they are seated, Jesus comes out and his opening words are "You bunch of snakes. You smell bad. You kind of remind me of decomposed bodies walking around. You're hypocrites and blind guides. And I want to thank you very much for coming." It was not exactly a speech that endeared the Pharisees to Jesus, which was what the disciples pointed out when they told him with a sudden flash of insight, "We think you might have offended them."

But for those who loved him he was equally exasperating. He constantly kept smashing some of his own followers' expectations of what the Messiah should do. He simply did not fit their mold. He did not try to. They thought the Messiah would come in power and liberate Jerusalem, in their Maccabean tradition. But the only power that Jesus demonstrated was the power of servanthood. His disciples wanted to know who would be first in terms of prestige. Jesus told them the first would be the greatest servant. For Jesus' greatness was seen not in the degree to which he was elevated, but the degree to which he came down and identified.

Even John the Baptist struggled with who Jesus was. He did not feel Jesus behaved as the Anointed One. John had taught that the Messiah would bring an age of judgment—but Jesus brought mercy. John felt the Messiah should separate himself from sinner and tax collector (like the prophets of the past) not invite them over for dinner.

Jesus put people into crisis by compelling them to do something. He commanded Peter to lower his nets for a catch of fish, after he had caught nothing all night. He told the rich young ruler to sell all his possessions. He told a Samaritan woman, whom he knew was living with another man, to go call her husband. He insisted that John baptize him when doing so would violate John's understanding of Messiah. He told the Pharisaical lawyer, who was far more interested in debate and discussion, to do what he understood and not to talk about it.

Jesus was a confident man. He was secure and he knew who he was. While other religious leaders were often self-effacing, Jesus was self-advancing. Other religious leaders often required their followers to obey rules or laws or "a way." Jesus said, "I am the way, and the truth, and the life" (Jn. 14:6). Based on that we are asked simply to follow him. Jesus didn't make suggestions, he uttered commands ("come to me," "follow me," "drop your nets"). I think we can safely say that Jesus was hardly the victim of a poor self-concept.

He was the Son of God. All these traits— his delightfulness, his compassion, his sensitivity, his passion, his ability to establish rapport as well as to exasperate—all sprang from the fundamental fact of his deity. He said he was the bread of life (Jn. 6:35), the light of the world (Jn. 8:12) and the resurrection and the life (Jn. 11:25). He said "I and the Father are one" (Jn. 10:30). He informed people that knowing him was the same as knowing God (Jn. 8:19), seeing him was the same as seeing God (Jn. 12:45), believing in him was the same as believing in God (Jn. 12:44) and receiving him was the same as receiving God (Mk. 9:37).

C. S. Lewis warned in *Mere Christianity* against the claim that Jesus was merely a good teacher but not the Son of God. John Stott also points out that Jesus could hardly have been a good teacher if he was so wrong about the chief subject of his teaching—namely, himself.

Let us suppose that I made the kind of claims that Jesus did and people began to say, "Isn't Becky terrific?! I mean, the way she forgives sins—she really has a style all of her own, doesn't she? And her moral ethics are so brilliant and impeccable! And what a superb teacher! . . . not to mention her perfect, sinless life. There is one little problem. She does seem to be a *little* confused about her deity. But other than that, she really has it all together!" Now whom do you think they would lock up first, the people saying this or me? No one is a little confused about his own deity and sane. Yet intelligent, well-meaning people say this about Jesus every day. So let us eliminate the option that Jesus was merely a good teacher. That was never left open to us.

But the continuing question that Jesus faced because of his claims and action was voiced the loudest by the Pharisees. They saw Jesus healing on the Sabbath and asked, "Who do you think you are?! Who do you think you are, healing on the Sabbath?" And Jesus answered, "The Lord of the Sabbath." There were no more questions.

Which leads me to my last impression of this towering figure. How did Jesus justify his behavior and claim that seemed to eventually lead everyone into conflict or crisis? I think it could be stated briefly like this; "I do what I do, because I am the Lord—and you are not. You follow me. I do not follow you." His answers were most often that simple. He said he was the Lord. He knew it. He lived like it. He acted like it. He wanted people to respond accordingly.

Jesus the Lord

3

A FEW YEARS AGO I WAS INVITED as part of a team to Stanford University to teach for a week on evangelism. I lived in a dorm with the students and on the first day I met Lois. She was bright and sensitive—and skeptical about the existence of God. After we had several talks about God, I told her I was having a Bible study for the floor, to look at the person of Jesus. She could come and examine the primary source material as critically as she would a Marxist manifesto.

"Okay, I'll come. But the Bible won't have anything relevant to say to me," she replied.

You Have No Husband

The next day I discovered Lois was living off campus with her boyfriend, Phil. To my great surprise he came with her to the Bible study. Not knowing her background, I had already decided to lead the study on the woman at the well in John 4. I began introducing the chapter to the group, noticed

Phil and Lois sitting there, and suddenly remembered the passage dealt with a woman who had sexual problems. I feared Lois would think I had planned this just for her.

With a step of faith, I frantically tried to think of how to avoid the crunch of the passage (though I was sure God had got me into this mess). Lois and Phil were seated close to my left. Thinking it would be better if Lois did not read the passage aloud, I called on Sally, who was immediately to my right, calculating that if each person read a paragraph aloud, we would finish before it was Lois's turn.

To my dismay a girl three seats away from Lois started reading. (I discovered later it was Sally's twin sister who happened to be sitting next to me.) Then Lois read the portion: "Jesus said to her, 'You are right in saying, "I have no husband" . . . for the man you're living with now is not your husband.'" It was her first experience of reading Scripture and her eyes grew as big as saucers, while I hid behind my Bible!

"I must say, this is a bit more relevant than I had expected," she commented with considerable understatement. And as she saw with what sensitivity and perception Jesus interacted with the lonely woman, Lois's face showed how moved she was.

The next day Lois and I talked again. "Is there any reason why you couldn't become a Christian?" I asked.

"No," she said.

"Well, I can think of one," I said. "What will you do about Phil?" Then we talked directly about how becoming a Christian isn't merely fire insurance; it's a relationship that affects every aspect of our lives: values, lifestyle, sexuality. As we talked, it became clear God had been pursuing her for a long time. There were tears and struggles followed by an utterly sincere prayer asking Christ to come into her life as Lord.

Immediately she said, "Becky, as a young Christian I've got problems. I'll have to tell Phil and move out; I have no place to go; it's impossible to get a dorm room this late, and now I'll have to pay this month's rent in two places." So we prayed again, and as she left my room I agonized over how such a young believer could handle so much.

After dinner the students who had attended the Bible study stopped me in the hall saying they were fascinated by the study on Jesus Christ. Then we heard a noise and turned to see what it was. Here came Lois, slowly walking down the corridor, carrying several suitcases and smiling with tears streaming down her cheeks. I silently thanked God. I too felt the tears slip down. Seldom have I seen a more graphic picture of what it means to become a Christian. Everyone began asking her why she had left home.

"Oh, no. I haven't left home. I've finally *found* my home," she replied. "You see, today I became a Christian."

That one decision had far-reaching effects. That same night three girls on the floor decided to get right with Christ. Another girl who had assumed she was a Christian realized she wanted no part of it if it demanded total commitment. The next day Lois was told she could move into a dorm (unheard of at such a late date), and she discovered her new roommate was a dynamic, mature Christian.

Three months later her boyfriend Phil became a Christian, and he too grew rapidly. He had been hostile over her conversion and furious with her for moving out. But after he was converted he told her, "Thanks, Lois, for loving God enough to put him first instead of me. Your obedience affected my eternal destiny."

Lois's conversion was profound for her friends as well as for her. She recognized that becoming a Christian had tremendous implications. She came to see that if Jesus is Lord then the only right response to him is surrender and obedience. He is Savior and he is Lord. We cannot separate his demands from his love. We cannot dissect Jesus and relate only to the parts that we like or need. Christ died so that we could be forgiven for managing our own lives. It would be impossible for Lois to thank Christ for dying for her and yet to continue running her own life.

She also saw that submitting her life to Jesus involved a cost. Jesus discouraged enthusiasts from committing themselves to him until they had weighed the implications. "Follow me," was his repeated command. "But there could be no following without a forsaking, a renunciation of competing loyalties, of personal ambition, of material possessions, of family relationships (Lk. 14:25-33)," John Stott writes. "Before a man could follow Jesus, he had to repudiate himself and his right to organize his own life."[1]

Why Jesus Is Lord

One may ask, what right does Jesus have to ask for so much? How can he get away with it? The biblical answer is: because he is the Lord. This is what the disciples preached ("What we preach is . . . Jesus Christ as Lord," 2 Cor. 4:5) and how they told us to live ("In your hearts reverence Christ as Lord," 1 Pet. 3:15). He is Lord because of who he is: God incarnate, Lord of creation and Lord of life.

First, Jesus is God incarnate. Colossians 1:15 tells us, "He is the image of the invisible God, the first-born of all creation." Hebrews 1:3 says, "He reflects the glory of God and bears the very stamp of his nature." And Colossians 2:9, "For in him the whole fulness of deity dwells bodily." Commenting on this text Dr. Martyn Lloyd-Jones says, "There is nothing beyond that. He is the sum total of all the Divine attributes and power."[2] C. S. Lewis puts it this way: "Then comes the real shock. Among these Jews there suddenly turns up a man who goes about talking as if He was God. He claims to forgive sin. He says He has always existed. He says He is coming to judge the world at the end of time. . . . And when you have grasped that, you will see that what this man said was, quite simply, the most shocking thing that has ever been uttered by human lips."[3]

Second, Jesus is Lord because of his relationship to the universe. He is the Lord of creation. Colossians 1:16-17 says, "For in him all things were created, in heaven and on earth, visible and invisible, whether thrones or dominions or principalities or authorities—all things were created through him and for him. He is before all things, and in him all things hold together." And Hebrews 1:3 teaches that by Christ all things consist. The Son is the agent of creation. He upholds "the universe by his word of power."

Third, Jesus revealed his authority over nature. Imagine the scene. The disciples and Jesus were in a boat headed for the shore. Jesus was sound asleep. There were expert and wily fishermen on board. Suddenly an awful storm arose. The wind and waves were so great that the boat began to sink. Experienced fishermen were alarmed. In desperation (and probably irritation at Jesus for sleeping and for suggesting they set out in the boat in the first place) they woke him up and said, "Teacher, do you not care if we perish?" And in the midst of this vicious storm and terrified passengers, Jesus casually got up, looked at the lake and said, " 'Peace! Be still!' And the wind ceased, and there was a great calm." If you think the disciples were feeling overwhelmed by the storm, think how they felt upon seeing this! "And they were filled with awe, and said to one another, 'Who then is this, that even wind and sea obey him?' " (Mk. 4:35-41).

Finally, Jesus is the Lord of life. "I am the Great Shepherd." "My sheep know my voice and I know their's." He created us. He understands human nature. He knows us thoroughly. He loves us and died for us. He is competent to direct our lives.

In the New Testament the lordship of Christ is no mere abstract principle. The Gospel writers illustrate as well as teach the principle. Mark does this through the idea of authority. Jesus began to teach and the people were astonished, "for he taught them as one who had authority, and not as the scribes" (Mk. 1:22). Jesus showed authority over the spirit world as he healed a demon-possessed man. And the people were amazed, saying, "With authority he commands even the unclean spirits, and they obey him" (Mk. 1:27). Jesus demonstrated authority over the physical body as he healed Peter's mother-in-law from illness (Mk. 1:31). And Jesus also revealed his authority over death by restoring the daughter of Jairus to life (Mk. 5:35-43). Jesus is Lord because of who he is.

Jesus also revealed his authority by forgiving sins (Mk. 2:1-12). Here he moves into dangerous territory for the people correctly realized one thing: "Why does this man speak thus? It is blasphemy. Who can forgive sins but God alone?" Jesus answered, "But that you may know that the Son of man has authority on earth to forgive sins, . . . I say to you, rise, take up your pallet and go home." And the people were all amazed, saying, "We never saw anything like this!"

Of course Lois did not realize the full extent to which Jesus is Lord. But she understood enough to know she could not follow him without obeying him. She either had to live under new management or forget about Jesus. I wish I could say that Lois is the norm. But all too often people say they believe in Jesus but their lifestyles betray their beliefs. Cathy, for instance.

Go Greyhound

As I boarded the bus for Willamette University in Salem, Oregon, I found myself sitting next to a rather nervous-looking young girl. As our conversation developed, she told me she was a Christian from a Christian home. Yet she looked frightened and lost, and as I began probing I discovered she was running away from home. She had used all of her money to buy a ticket to Salem; from there she planned to hitchhike to California. She had no money, she hadn't eaten for a while and she was afraid.

We discussed her inability to get along with her parents among other personal problems. When I asked how her faith in Christ affected her decision to leave home, I was disappointed by her impoverished understanding of what it meant to be a Christian. At no point did she mention Christ's lordship in her life, only that he was a "neat feeling in my heart." As we talked about who Jesus Christ is and how he is Lord as well as Savior, she decided she wasn't willing for him to have that much control, though she fully believed he is God.

After arriving in Salem, I persuaded Cathy to let me buy her lunch, and during the next hour I prayed fervently as she insisted on continuing her trip. I had previously scheduled appointments with students all day, but by merely observing me with her in the student union they sensed the situation and realized I needed prayer. So they quietly prayed at several tables while I continued to talk with her.

Suddenly at 12:15 Cathy looked at me in surprise and said, "I can't believe I'm saying this—but I'm going to go home. And not because you want me to, or because I want to, but because I've decided to mean business with God. If Christ is going to be Lord of my life, then he'll have to call the shots and he'll help me work out my family problems." We rejoiced and thanked God together as she committed her life to Christ in a new and total way.

Then I tried to catch up on my appointments while Cathy called her parents. She was certain they wouldn't have seen the farewell note yet. To her disappointment her mother answered the telephone weeping because they had found the note and were frantic with worry. They had gone immediately to their knees in prayer asking God to protect her and bring her back. (They began praying, I discovered later, five minutes before her decision to return.) Then Cathy told them she had meant to run away from home, but "God put this Christian right next to me on the bus—it was spooky!" I laughed as she described me as "this girl who goes from one school to the next and just talks about God—all day long—and she even gets paid for it!" It was evident that God wanted her parents to read the note in order to bring healing in their relationships not only to God but to each other as well.

I put Cathy on the bus and with a radiant face she thanked us all. (By now all of the Christians in the union were "in" on this drama!) I thought that would be the end of this episode, but there is an exciting sequel.

One month later Katey Finney, an associate of Inter-Varsity Christian Fellowship in Portland, was sitting on a city bus next to an older woman. When this woman discovered Katey worked with Inter-Varsity, she said, "I love I-V! One of their workers sat next to my runaway daughter, and she came back home to us. Consequently we talked and really listened to her, and we just sent her to California for a vacation. But as a result of that crisis, I realized I need to grow more in God. I feel I'm stagnating. Do you think we could meet again?"

The amusing thing is that a Greyhound bus driver who was a Christian heard the story and shared it at the Christian bus drivers' monthly meeting. (I didn't know such a group existed!) Later I was told that it had been an inspiration to them all and they were grateful that I "go Greyhound." Perhaps I should have asked for a "spiritual discount"!

A Question of Control

Two things concern me about Cathy and so many young Christians I meet. I am distressed by a frighteningly debased view of truth. Many students may be convinced Christianity is true, but the truth of something doesn't seem to have any binding consequences. Second, there seems to be almost a disease of superficiality in their faith. This stems, I fear, from our impoverished understanding of what it means to call Jesus Lord.

We are sometimes so anxious to get our friends across the goal line that we fail to present a clear and honest picture of Christianity. Unless seekers clearly understand the gospel, both its costs and privileges, before they commit themselves to God, our harvest will be poor indeed. We must communicate that salvation is clearly tied to a relationship to the living Christ as *Lord* as well as Savior; it is tied to objective truth that demands a total response. Warm feelings and shivers are not enough; they are not even required.

Lois was perhaps unusual in recognizing quickly the tie between belief in Christ and the necessity of integrating him into her life. Cathy believed in Jesus but she failed to integrate his person into her life. If we fail to integrate, what does that say about our spiritual beliefs in the first place? What does it mean, then, to allow Jesus to be the Lord of our lives? What does it mean that anything is the lord of our life?

Just this: Whatever controls us is our lord. The person who seeks power is controlled by power. The person who seeks acceptance is controlled by the people he or she wants to please. We do not control ourselves. We are controlled by the lord of our life. If Jesus is our Lord, then he is the one who controls, he has the ultimate power. There are no bargains. We cannot manipulate him by playing "let's make a deal." If he is Lord, the only option open to us is to do his will, to let him have control. Jesus remains Lord whether we accept him or not. His lordship, his essence, is not affected by what we choose. But our lives are drastically changed by our choice.

It is not a control that manipulates us or takes away our dignity. Jesus never presumes things or decides things for people. He does not abuse or bully people. In fact we find Jesus asking as many questions as people asked him. He does not decide what people need and then give it to them. He asked the blind beggar Bartimaeus, "What do you want me to do for you?" (Mk. 10:51). He asked the paralytic, "Do you want to be healed?" (Jn. 5:6). He asked Peter, "Who do you say that I am?" (Mt. 16:15), "Do you love me?" (Jn. 21:15) and "Do you also wish to go away?" (Jn. 6:67). And he told his disciples, "If you love me, you will keep my commandments" (Jn. 14:15).

Jesus always preserves our freedom. He allows us to choose him over all others. Jesus will not control us in the wrong way.

Nor will he control us in the easy way, by making every decision for us. He controls us in the right way: by being who he is without compromise and by insisting we become all that we are meant to be. And he tells us this can occur only through following him, obeying him and maintaining a living, passionate, stormy kinship to him.

We are to reflect Christ and obey him not only because of who he is but because of who we have become. The very nature of God dwells in us now. As Oswald Chambers has said, "Jesus is ruthless in His demands and uncompromising because He has put into us the very nature of God."[4]

Summarizing God's purpose for human beings, the Westminster Shorter Catechism tells us that we are created to glorify God and enjoy him forever. God created us for himself. If we are living with any center other than Jesus, we will be living incompletely. So Jesus continually tries to help people see who or what controls them. That is why Jesus is far more interested in people's lives than in their God-talk. Your life, more than your words, will reveal what really controls you.

Jesus aimed for the jugular vein in his conversations. He knew that faith meant submitting to his authority, not merely getting him to do what we want. Jesus knew people liked him, enjoyed him, thought he was stimulating and really desired for him to be on their team. Jesus also knew that those are not the rules of the game.

There are problems in this issue of control. Either we are controlled by the wrong thing, or we try to control Jesus by limiting him to our terms. Jesus will accept our faith but he will never accept our controls.

People struggled as much with the "control problem" in the first century as we do today. For example, the rich young ruler (Mk. 10:17-22) was a man who cared for God—a man who was religious and conscientious but who at heart was controlled by something other than God. "And Jesus looking upon him

loved him," and said to him, "Go, sell what you have, and give
to the poor." Jesus wanted him to see that what was funda-
mentally controlling him was not the love of God but the love
of money. Likewise, he told the Pharisees it was tradition that
controlled them (Mk. 7:9).

Jesus also refused to let others control him. In Luke, Satan
is the first person who tried to control Jesus (Lk. 4:1-13). Jesus
had been in the wilderness for forty days without eating. So
Satan first tempted him with food. But Jesus refused to let his
stomach have ultimate control over him. In exchange for
worshiping him, the devil then offered Jesus power, the
power of all the kingdoms of the world. But Jesus refused to
be controlled by power. Satan tried to persuade Jesus to tempt
God, and that too failed.

Then Satan tempted Jesus in one other profound way. He
tested Jesus at the point of his identity. He began, "*If* you are
the Son of God...." Jesus had just heard his Father say,
"Thou art my beloved son" at his baptism. But he was hungry
and tired. Perhaps Satan thought this was the best place to
begin.

How did Jesus handle this temptation about his identity?
He did not answer, "You know it's funny you'd bring that up
today. I'm not feeling very well and I'm so hungry. Maybe we
should discuss it. Let me sit here and introspect a while to see if
I really feel like God's Son. Maybe I could check a commen-
tary or reread that book I brought along on self-realization."
Jesus' answer was "It is written." What was the basis of Jesus'
understanding of reality? Was it his feeling on a particular
day? No. Jesus derived his sense of identity from his
relationship to God and from the written Word of God.

If Satan attacked Jesus first at the level of his identity, we
can expect a similar assault. Jesus shows us that our self-image,
our sense of worth, our understanding of who we are must be
rooted in God's Word. How we happen to feel about ourselves
on a particular morning has nothing to do with it. It is not

God that gives us the message that we are worthless or inadequate. Such tactics belong to someone else. God tells the people of Israel, "You are precious in my eyes, and honored, and I love you" (Is. 43:4). True, he also tells us that we are sinners, but that is far from saying we are insignificant.

Other enemies tried to control Jesus. Judas probably thought he had power over Jesus. But Jesus told Judas, "What you are going to do, do quickly" (Jn. 13:27). He not only knew of the death plot but he told Judas when to leave and how to do it. When Jesus did not answer Pilate's interrogation before his death, Pilate said, in a vein of thought not unlike Satan's temptation in the wilderness, "Do you not know that I have power to release you, and power to crucify you?" (Jn. 19:10). Jesus replied that the only way Pilate could have power over him would be if God gave it to him.

Even Jesus' own family tried to control him. When people thought he had gone mad, his family tried to persuade him to come home (Mk. 3:21). Later, they suggested he go and preach at the Feast of the Tabernacles. Jesus knew why. The Jews sought to kill him there (Jn. 7:1-5).

In the moment of greatest popularity he would not allow the people to subtly control him by making him king (Jn. 6:15). Neither would he allow the Pharisees to arrest and kill him prematurely (Jn. 8:59; 10:39), nor could the Pharisees control him with their many questions and tests (for example, Lk. 11:16-26; Mk. 8:1-13; Jn. 8:6).

Jesus' disciples struggled as much with him as his enemies did. It began over smaller issues but led into much more dramatic ones. Peter and his friends found Jesus praying and told him urgently, "Every one is searching for you" (Mk. 1:37). They expected him to stay and heal others. But Jesus resisted their pressure and told them they were to move on to a new town so he could preach.

Jesus told Peter to lower his nets for a catch of fish. Peter probably thought it was absurd for a carpenter to give fishing

directions to him, an experienced fisherman, particularly
when he had been out fishing all night and had caught
nothing. One cannot help but hear Peter's exasperation if not
his sarcasm when he loudly announces, "Master, we toiled all
night and took nothing! But at *your word* I will let down
the nets" (Lk. 5:5). Peter did not want the other men to think
it was his idea! Peter's abject response, "Depart from me,
for I am a sinful man, O Lord," (v. 8) reveals how deeply,
though silently, he had resisted Jesus' idea in the first
place.

When Jesus began to wash Peter's feet in John 13, Peter
again disagreed with Jesus. Jesus should never do so low and
menial a task as that! But Jesus insisted and provided a much
needed model for Peter that leaders must not only serve, but
allow others to serve them as well.

But most traumatic for Peter was Jesus' death. It would
have been far easier for Peter if Jesus had tried to flee but had
been finally captured by his enemies, sentenced and hanged.
Peter had expected Jesus to liberate Jerusalem in the great
Maccabean tradition. He had staked everything on that. So
when the soldiers came to arrest Jesus, he did what he thought
was necessary. He sliced off the soldier's ear in an attempt to
usher in the kingdom of God with a sword. Jesus said he had a
different idea for liberation. He would die. Peter disagreed
violently. How could one liberate anything by dying? To die
means the cause is over, not that it has begun! Later Peter
denied the Lord three times. Was it simply out of cowardice,
or because he disagreed with his strategy as well?

So, what is the point of all this? Jesus accepted Peter's faith,
but he would not accept his controls. Peter had to learn again
and again that when he and Jesus disagreed, Peter was the one
who would have to change.

Why was Jesus so uncompromising? He said he was Lord.
He also said that what controlled him was his Father's will (Jn.
5:19-20). He always obeyed him (Jn. 5:30; 8:29) and there-

fore never allowed people to control his character or his message.

There was one thing about Jesus that people were able to control, however. They could, in a limited way, control Jesus' effectiveness. He sternly charged a leper to tell no one who had healed him. But because the leper went out and spoke freely, Jesus could no longer openly enter that city (Mk. 1:43-45). When Jesus came to his home town and taught, the townspeople were amazed by his wisdom and miracles. But they "took offense at him" for they remembered him as the carpenter's son. Their children had grown up with Jesus. And Jesus could not do a mighty work there and "he marveled because of their unbelief" (Mk. 6:1-6). Jesus will not take away our freedom, even when it condemns us and hinders him.

Whether people tried to control Jesus or were controlled by something other than him, his message was constant. He must be the center of our life, the controlling force. Why? Because he says he is the bread of life (Jn. 6:35). He is the essential. He is not dessert, but the very substance of life. He says he is *the* door (Jn. 10:7). He is not *a* door, or an *interesting* door if you did not happen to take the elevator. He is the only door.

Sooner or later nearly everyone became exasperated with Jesus. They tried to manipulate him, trick him and limit him. But everyone had to learn what Peter did. Jesus is Lord and they were not.

The first century was prone to limiting Christ's lordship, either by trying to control Jesus to meet their expectations or by being controlled by the wrong thing. But how do we limit Jesus in the twentieth century? Earl Palmer, the pastor of First Presbyterian Church in Berkeley, California, has suggested four limitations in an address he gave in Portland, Oregon. He has now developed them in his book *Love Has Its Reasons*.[5] I would like to elaborate on these.

The Limitations of Christ

First, we limit Christ by wanting an eros-experience with God. Frequently I ask non-Christian students what they think would happen if they were to meet Jesus and allow him to be Lord of their lives. And I ask Christian students how they expect to mature spiritually, how they determine whether to go to a weekend retreat and so forth. Both sources all too frequently give the same response. The non-Christians sooner or later communicate they will become a Christian when they are overwhelmed by God. They expect God to stun them so totally with his power and love that they will be left speechless, their senses dazzled. Christians often say they will go to a conference or accept a position of spiritual leadership on campus if God really "zaps" them. When they go to conferences, it is clear they will be disappointed unless the speaker lifts them out of their seats. Both sides are asking for the same thing, a high to beat all highs, a trip to beat all trips.

Why do we want these ecstatic experiences? Rollo May, a well-known psychiatrist, correctly says it is because we live in an "eros-oriented" society. The Greek word *eros* translated most accurately means to be attracted to some person or thing by its compelling beauty. We see the object's excellence and beauty and our wills are simply swept away and we are overwhelmed.

Palmer argues forcefully that we want an eros-experience with God. We want our wills stamped out, our decision-making process obliterated. Why? So that we will have no other choice but to believe! God has the power to do this, but he usually will not. Such is C. S. Lewis's point in *Screwtape Letters* when he has the senior devil below write to his ambassador devil Wormwood on earth: "You must have often wondered why the Enemy [God] does not make more use of His power to be sensibly present to human souls in any degree He chooses and at any moment. But you now see that the Irresistible and the Indisputable are the two weapons which the very nature of His scheme forbids Him to use."[6]

Jesus is not a vibe, an emotion, an energy or the ultimate trip that will overwhelm our senses. He is the Lord. He wants to give us his love—but it must be given because we have responded to his call, his invitation, not because we were overwhelmed. He offers us his journeying presence, not a series of ecstatic experiences every three minutes in order to get us to obey. We must examine our lives, our fellowships, our churches and ask, Do we want an emotional high before we are willing to follow Jesus? If we are waiting only for the "warm fuzzies," we may be waiting for a long time.

Second, we limit Jesus by seeing him as "the answer" to our problems. William Stringfellow has written that many people like to treat Jesus as the answer to their problems or needs or causes. That is why they are Christians. Indeed, in one way Jesus very likely is the answer. His presence does bring comfort to a poor self-image, to a divorced home situation, to feelings of desperate loneliness. But we must never forget that Jesus is always larger than our problems or causes. And if Jesus is only the answer to our problems, then we still have control over him because he can only be an answer to what we determine the problem to be. He becomes our God of the gaps.

Here is the danger. If we follow Jesus only because he helps us with such problems as loneliness, then what happens on the day when we again feel desperately alone? Do we cease to follow him and obey? Or what if we get therapy and our problem is resolved? Is he no longer Lord now that we do not "need" him to bring comfort in that area?

Or perhaps Jesus has driven me to fight for a cause, to fight injustice and to protect human dignity. I would be disobedient not to respond to the call. But I would be equally disobedient to make Jesus merely the leader of my cause. Though he calls us to a cause, he is always larger than the cause. Jesus breaks through our expectations and problems and causes and molds, and he declares he is Lord over against our most noble causes and gripping needs.

We follow Jesus because he is in truth the Lord, the living God. He is not just an experience to cheer us up on a bad day, or merely the fighter of our cause. He is much larger and much more radical than that.

Third, we limit Jesus by reducing his claims. We begin to see how vast Jesus' claims are. We see what he is calling us to and how high and uncompromising his standards are. Then we also see how far we are from what he is calling us to be. We recognize there is a great gap between his moral demands and our behavior. So we try to narrow this gap by reducing his claims.

For example, Jesus tells us to love our enemies (Mt. 5:44). So we think, "Isn't that nice. I just love religious mottos. They always have such a ring to them. Maybe I'll put it up on my wall." It sounds great . . . until you think of an enemy. Then comes the crunch. "How could I possibly *love* that person? She wants to do me in! Why, to love her goes completely against my grain. Jesus could not possibly be asking me to do that! When Jesus said, 'Love your enemies,' what he *really* meant was, if you see them coming down the street don't trip them or punch them out; just walk down the other side of the street. Obviously he did not mean love in the sense that we think of it. He could not mean that because it is just too hard to do."

Do you see? We try to solve the problem of the mighty claims of Jesus by reducing him to our limits. We soften him to accommodate us. And the result and the irony is that as we lose the offense of Jesus' absolute radical claims we also lose his appeal.

I remember as a non-Christian looking for the first time at the Gospels. I was offended by how uncompromising Jesus was. And yet I was intrigued and drawn for the same reason. He did not sound like he was on the losing team. If our Jesus ends up sounding only like the Great Sweet Friend of America we have lost before we begin. "Listen, I know how tired you get. And all this stuff about loving your enemy. Do you think I would have said that if I had known your roommate? And this sex stuff really is a bit Victorian. I tell you what: you just go do your thing and, like your dog, I'll be here when you need me."

That may be how some see Jesus, but that is not the Jesus of the Gospels. He is Lord. The paradox remains that the more uncompromising he is the more appeal he has.

Fourth, we limit Jesus by trying to elevate ourselves. Another way we try to reconcile the great gap that exists between God's standards and our behavior is by glorifying ourselves. We see the vast difference between Jesus and ourselves and we pretend the gap doesn't exist. We overspiritualize and pretend there is no struggle.

I met a Christian recently whose remarks made me feel like a washout for having struggles. Her attitude was something like this: "What—*me* struggle? Why, I just follow Jesus. It's so easy. I fly from victory to victory. Ah, the joys of the abundant life! Why, I'm about as saccharine as you could possibly stomach. Just let the nominal stay down there and struggle. I'll just live in the world of the triumphant."

I love ebullient people. But there was something unreal about her. Every other phrase was "praise God" whether it fit or not. She seemed incapable of dealing with anything negative or painful; all she knew was victory. It is not that I wanted her to have problems. Rather, I was not sure that she was living in reality. The kind of attitude that denies struggle or conflict not only will not work, it will never attract people. It is a dangerous presumption not to admit that we live amidst crisis. We are sinners and in desperate and constant need of God's grace.

In fact, it is the very claims of Jesus himself that prevent us from overspiritualizing and force us to be human. If we say, "Oh, I just love everybody. I never struggle with people now that I follow Jesus," we have a problem. For Jesus said, "Love your enemies," and he would not ask us to love something that we did not have. Jesus certainly *does* want us to love all people. He does not want us to seek out an enemy just so we can obey his command to love them! But he is realistic. He knows we are sinners and there will be people that we do not like and that do not like us. The issue as a Christian is not to *pretend* that we love everything that moves and breathes. That would be phoney and hypocritical. Jesus does not tell us to pretend they are friends either. Rather he asks that we acknowledge the fact that they are enemies without pretense and yet to respond to them with love, not hate or bitterness.

There is tremendous freedom in this. I am given the freedom to be honest before God about how I feel about a person. But my *response* must reflect what God is like, which will lead eventually to my healing as well. His command calls me to honesty (which is never overly spiritual), but it does not celebrate or justify my negative feelings. He gives me the freedom to acknowledge my negative attitudes before him but not the freedom to act them out because they are as destructive for me as they are for the other person.

The apostle Paul counsels, "Do not let the sun go down on your anger" (Eph. 4:26). Judging by some Christians' behavior, I would have thought Jesus' departing words were, "Never get angry. But if you do, for heaven's sake, pretend you aren't and fake it." But that is wrong. Jesus does not encourage destructive anger, but neither does he ask us to pretend it doesn't exist. The point is to deal with our anger. We are to resolve the conflict and seek reconciliation the very day it occurs. To deny the reality of sin or struggle in our lives is to deny God the opportunity of working through our weakness.

Christ Unlimited

Gene Thomas once said something very freeing for me. You realize, he said, who Jesus is and how radical and uncompromising his claims are. Then he begins to speak to you about an area that he doesn't have control over yet. You're not stupid, you know what is involved, and you know your own limits. You say to yourself, "That's the nuttiest thing I've ever heard of. I don't want to do it. It's crazy." But it is when you begin to fight and sweat that you begin the process of being a disciple.

Christianity isn't a narcotic that dulls you into obedience. It involves battle—it's excruciating to give up control. But that is why we must not feel despair if we are struggling. To struggle does not mean we are incorrigible. It means we are *alive!*

A disciple says, "I hear you. It's the nuttiest thing I ever heard of. It's risky. I'll look like a fool, but I'll do it. Because my life is no longer committed to doing my thing but your thing." Heaven will not be filled with innocent people, running around saying, "Oh, was there another way? I guess I never noticed." Rather they will say, "You bet there were other options that begged to control me. By God's grace and my struggle, Jesus is my Lord."

Is Jesus' desire to be the Lord of our lives some little fetish of his? Why is it so important to him? Why should we want him to have control of our lives? Besides the fact that he deserves it because of who he is, he knows he is the only one in the universe who can control us without destroying us. No one will ever love you like Jesus. No one will ever know you better, care more for your wholeness and pull more for you. You don't need fifteen years of analysis to discover you are unrepeatable. The last breath Jesus breathed on this planet was for you. Jesus will meet you wherever you are and he will help you. He is not intimidated by past failures, broken promises or wounds. He will make sense out of your brokenness. But he can only begin to be the Lord of your life today, not next Monday or next month, but now.

And the great and joyful paradox is that while he totally transforms us he makes us more ourselves than ever before.

A Question of Priority:
Jesus and the Pharisees

4

A STUDENT WHO EARNESTLY desired to share Christ's love with his friends told me, "Don't give me any new formulas to witness naturally. I've tried everything. It just doesn't seem right to use surveys of steps on someone you know."

This student is typical of many. Christians say they want to communicate their faith naturally instead of seeming artificial or contrived. So in their pursuit of this, they investigate every witnessing technique on the spiritual market.

"I'm not going to suggest a new formula," I said, "because I feel as you do that techniques aren't the most effective, especially for friends. Have you ever thought about looking more deeply at the life of Jesus? If you live by the same values and priorities he had, you will find evangelism happening naturally. It becomes a lifestyle and not a project."

When we develop a way of living that places a special emphasis on people, that demonstrates holiness and a dedicated obedience to God, we can't help but be an effective witness. Evangelism will flow from our lives instead of from memorized techniques.

But this puts the burden on us. What did Jesus value? What did he place priority on? What was his notion of holiness? What role does obedience play?

We can answer these questions by looking at Jesus' conflict with the Pharisees. And that will help us understand the traps and boxes we, too, so frequently fall into.

Who Were the Pharisees?

The study of the Pharisees is complex. For one thing, there is a marked contrast between the picture of the Pharisees given in the Gospels and that found in later rabbinical records. It is also difficult to know the exact nature of Judaism in Jesus' day.[1] I want to give as fair and accurate a picture as possible of the Pharisees, but also want to deal directly with Jesus' criticism of them.

I fully accept Jesus' charges against those who criticized him. But I am uneasy saying his criticism characterized the movement as a whole. There were some Pharisees who followed Jesus (most likely Nicodemus was one). There were others who were probably left unmentioned. So when addressing the problems of the Pharisees, I am not speaking about the movement as a whole. Rather I am referring to those who criticized Jesus.

The Pharisees have received a lot of bad press. But we must not forget that they were a lay movement who cared deeply about God. They probably had more in common with Jesus than any other theological school of his time, yet they were his severest critics. Louis Finklestein says they were people who were drawn from the tradesmen of the town, not like the Sadducees who were descendants of the patrician landowners.[2] They were popular and held in esteem by the people at large.

The derivation of their name is uncertain, although F. F. Bruce suggests, "It is . . . likely that they were called 'Phari-

sees' in the sense of 'separatists' because of their strict avoid-
ance of everything which might convey ceremonial impurity
to them."[3] The Pharisees were devoted to maintaining the
Levitical laws of purity concerning ritual, food and the Sabbath. They were scrupulous about tithing the produce of the
soil (Lk. 18:12; Mt. 23:23) as well as evangelizing faithfully.
They believed that by studying and obeying the law and the
Tradition of the Elders they could strictly avoid ceremonial
impurity.

They shared many of Jesus' beliefs. "They took seriously
the biblical doctrine of God's government of the universe and
overruling of the actions of men for the furtherance of his
own purpose," writes Bruce. "And . . . there was no difference
between them with regard to the limits of holy writ, it was on
their interpretation that they disagreed."[4] They also shared a
belief in the resurrection of the body and the existence of
angels.

The Pharisees fanatically studied the law, and in doing so
they built up a body of traditional interpretation and application. Eventually their tradition became as sacrosanct as the
law itself. They were traditionalists even more than literalists.
Later generations of rabbis taught that the oral law was revealed to Moses at the same time as the written law on Sinai.
Indeed the Sanhedrin (which did not represent total consensus among the Pharisees) taught that it is more culpable to
teach contrary to precepts of the scribes than to teach contrary to the Torah itself.[5]

Why did the Pharisees build up an elaborate ceremonial
code? There are no conclusive answers to that question. W. D.
Davies argues that the Pharisees built up their Tradition of
the Elders out of a deep desire to make the Mosaic Law applicable to life.[6] They did not want to be like the Sadducees
who believed literally in the law and would accept no outside
source as authoritative. But Moses received the law over a
thousand years before. The present conditions Israel faced

were widely different, and that made relevant application of
the law difficult. So the Sadducees could claim to serve God, to
hold a literalistic view of the law, while rigidly maintaining the
status quo. Davies states that out of the Pharisees' attempt to
bring the whole of life under control of the law they adopted
the even more complex code of purification and separation.
By examining and expounding the law, they sought to find
the right conduct and to prescribe it for every circumstance in
life. Every iota was covered and nothing was left to chance.
While the Greeks approached all sciences with the question,
"What is real?" the Jews approached all sciences with the
question, "What is right?" "They did not ask, 'What is more
convenient' . . . but, 'What is God's pleasure?' "[7]

However noble and sincere the Pharisees' motives may have
been, they were still harshly criticized by Jesus for honoring
the tradition of men over the law of God. Cranfield comments, "The Tradition of the Elders pretended to be a fence,
to protect the Law from infringement, but in actual fact it
tampered with the Law. Jesus charges the Pharisees and the
Scribes with actually disobeying the Law of God through the
extravagant reverence of the Oral Law. . . . It was their interpretation, their tradition which was at fault; for it clung to the
letter of the particular passage in such a way as to miss the
meaning of Scripture as a whole."[8]

Let us look at three areas in which Jesus and the Pharisees
greatly differed: what they regarded as important, what it
means to be holy and what it means to know and obey God. All
three of these areas are vital in evangelism. We will deal with
the first of these in the present chapter and the other two in
the two chapters that follow.

What the Pharisees Regarded as Important
The Pharisees were sticklers about obeying the ceremonial
laws. They knew God called them to obedience and they
sought to devote themselves wholeheartedly to the Levitical

laws of purity.

The basic problem of the Pharisees, it appears, was that most were less concerned with the prophets (Hosea, Amos, Isaiah, etc.) than they were with the priestly ceremonial laws (Deuteronomy, Leviticus, etc.).The Pharisees who criticized Jesus seemed concerned only with the laws concerning separation and purification. They took their Tradition of the Elders as nearly sacrosanct itself. Their preoccupation was in not breaking their laws; no small task, as their laws were ever increasing.

They had laws concerning whether one should praise a bride extravagantly (which this writer thinks is a marvelous idea!) and laws on how to greet a bereaved person. There were laws for preventive medicine, such as the law that said no woman could look in the mirror on the Sabbath. The rabbis feared she might discover a gray hair and yank it out, thus performing work.

What was the result of their exclusive emphasis on obeying the ceremonial laws of purity and their seeming neglect of the moral law—what Jesus called the "weightier matters of the law, justice and mercy and faith" (Mt. 23:23)? It fed and eagerly encouraged the already existing social hierarchy. Their fervor for ceremonial purity led to an apartheid response to almost anyone who was not a part of their exclusive sect. There was strict separation from Gentiles, from Samaritans and even an aloofness from fellow Jews who did not have the time or leisure to study the law as they did. The Pharisees desired solidarity with the educated, powerful and wise, and utter separation from the rest.

Within their social hierarchy the most learned of the law were the most revered; the unlearned were the most despised. Consequently there was no gospel to the lost. Instead they assumed that those "who do not know the law, are accursed" (Jn. 7:49).

What Jesus Regarded as Important

Jesus smashed the Pharisees' notion that religious activity was what was really pleasing to God. Through both his life and his teaching, he proclaimed that the only way to please God was through proper relationships.

Jesus was wholly concerned with God and wholly concerned with people. That is, according to Jesus the human cause is God's cause. His lifestyle rose out of the simple truth of loving God, our neighbors and ourselves. His life was a constant celebration of the supreme value, dignity and preciousness of human life.

Malcolm Muggeridge once wrote, "That there is more joy in heaven over one sinner who repents is an antistatistical proposition." Jesus had an antistatistical approach to people. He loved sinners. He demonstrated that everyone is someone to God. There were no little people, no hierarchy. He was not impressed with a pecking order (Mk. 10:42-45) but with servanthood (Jn. 13:1-20). He identified with the unimportant, the weak and sinful, the poor and powerless. And because he identified with them, to his critics he became one. At his resurrection the first to witness his appearance were women, the powerless in his culture.

He once met a blind beggar, Bartimaeus (Mk. 10:46-52). To everyone but Jesus, Bartimaeus was an insignificant pauper who wanted to interrupt the schedule of the king. But Jesus stopped everything and asked the people who had shouted at the beggar to get lost, to call him to Jesus. Jesus not only served this beggar; he asked those who considered him insignificant to serve him too. What a humiliation for them!

Jesus took time to talk to children and to hold them (Mk. 10:13-16). Children seemed to have a habit of crashing his meetings with adults. The disciples scolded them and told them to go away. After all, this was *the* Jesus they were trying to see, a very busy and important man. But Jesus scolded the adults and told them their values were wrong. The disciples thought only "important people" should see Jesus. It took them a long time to understand that for Jesus, any person was of supreme importance.

The teaching that life is relationship did not begin with Jesus. It is a fundamental biblical principle. To be is to be in relation to someone. The Trinity evidences this. In Genesis we see that God sought relationship with us. Then he gave Adam a mate because "it is not good that the man should be alone" (Gen. 2:18). It is interesting to note that modern psychology is turning away from seeing mental health in terms of solitary individuals and viewing it in terms of the adequacy of human relationships. This new approach is in some ways a return to the ancient Hebrew-Christian understanding.

Why did Jesus so stress and demonstrate the necessity of a life that bears the stamp of profound love? Jesus said it reveals his Father's essence. Jesus was not loving and kind to others merely because he happened to be warm and considerate and had good role models at home. He loved people the way he did because he was doing his Father's will and demonstrating his character. He taught the Pharisees (and his disciples) that God has an extravagant endless kind of love for people.

Royalty in Rags

In one exchange with the Pharisees (who were very troubled by Jesus' contact with sinners), Jesus painted the bleakest possible picture of their understanding of a sinner. He told the story of a Jewish boy who insulted his father, left home and squandered all his money on immoral living. If that was not bad enough, he got so hungry that he found a job tending pigs. (What was a nice, orthodox Jewish boy doing around swine?) But then Jesus went one step further. This boy, no doubt raised in a kosher kitchen, got so hungry he wanted to eat pigs' food! Imagine the orthodox crowd's response to this wretched story. And finally the boy became so hungry that he decided to go back to his father because he was sorry and he knew his father would feed him. Hardly the most abject repentance we have ever read about!

And what was the father's response? Jesus has given us one of the most moving pictures of God in the New Testament. He told the Pharisees that even while the son was a long way off the father saw him, broke into a run, and with outstretched arms embraced him, kissed him and proceeded to dress him like a king. He did not care about getting his robes dirty. The boy had come home and that was all that mattered. It was time to celebrate and the father threw a party.

Suppose a neighbor were to walk by this scene. Let's imagine this is what happened. He doesn't know that the father has just bestowed clothes and jewelry upon the boy. He sees the father standing with a guest garbed in an ornate robe used only for very special guests, usually royalty. Then as the young man gestures with his hand, the neighbor sees a jeweled ring sparkling in the sunlight. He notices sandals on his feet and a fatted calf being prepared for a feast. Then it hits him. The young man must be a prince! All the details add up. The robe—the ring—the festivity and excitement.

The neighbor wants desperately to go over and say hello—if only he could get up his nerve. But he is only a commoner, a nobody. Yet the father who owns the house seems so kind and generous that the neighbor decides to drop in for a minute and sneak in a hello. Maybe he can even get the guest's autograph. He slowly creeps up behind the two men. The father's arm is still around the shoulders of the younger man as they walk. They talk but mostly the father listens intently to the young man. His eyes are wise and kind, and occasionally they brim—it seems for joy. The neighbor thinks he has never seen anyone as delighted to see another person.

He decides that if the father is that excited to see this man, then he must be a *very* important person. So he approaches the two men and speaks hesitantly, asking if he can have the privilege of meeting this most honored guest. The father nearly bursts with pride and delight. The father would love for him to meet his guest. Slowly the beautifully robed young man turns around. But what the neighbor sees frightens him so that he nearly jumps back in disgust. For there in these beautiful robes, exquisite jewelry and sandals, is a young man who looks half dead. He is grimy, unshaven and smelly. His face is sunken and his jaundiced skin seems to barely hang over his bones. He looks diseased. The neighbor begins to feel a bit nauseous and makes a quick excuse to leave. The father is so full of joy that he scarcely notices that his uninvited guest has left abruptly.

Jesus made profound statements in his story. One is that all of us look like that prodigal son when we stand next to the Father. We all look diseased. But when we come to God and become his children, he dresses us in his royal robes of righteousness. The exciting thing Jesus teaches here is that once we come to him, once we belong to him, we are royalty walking on the earth. All of us have specks of his royal gold in us. We are all made in his image. That image has been marred, but never so marred that the specks of gold have been obliterated. And never so marred that God by his grace cannot redeem us and adopt us as his own special heirs. When we go out into the world we ought never forget that we are interacting with potential royalty. We may be conversing with an heir apparent.

Jesus revealed to the Pharisees the nature of God and the tremendous value he places on human life. He also made a powerful statement about the depth and magnitude of God's love for one disease-ridden sinful person. Jesus reached out to others in love and asks us to do likewise because we are called to mirror the nature of God himself. This is not a call to be affectionate and affable and sweet because it is such a nice thing to do. It is a call to love as God loves.

So deeply did Jesus stress the importance of having a love relationship that he said if we are at the altar and realize we are not at peace with a person, we are to quit doing anything religious. We are to leave the altar and become reconciled to that person (Mt. 5:23). Jesus went further and said we are to love the unlovely, our enemies (Mt. 5:44). We are to love those who do not know the law, not curse them. God's love in us must extend across all boundaries.

A Neighbor's Love

Jesus also taught about the call to relationship in his conversation with the lawyer in Luke 10:25-37. An intellectual lawyer had come to Jesus with a rather ponderous question, "What shall I do to inherit eternal life?" This reminds me of the five delightful years I worked with Inter-Varsity Christian Fellowship at Reed College in Portland, Oregon. Reed students have a mentality all of their own. They are brilliant, intense, verbose; they love spending hour after hour discussing ideas. They are devoted to study. They love probing the sublime, the esoteric and the metaphysical. The more obscure it is, the better they like it, just so long as it seldom touches reality. Practical questions are considered a bit gauche, direct answers unfortunate and simplistic. They would far rather probe for the rare esoteric pearls. The longer I have studied Pharisaical lawyers the more I am convinced that the man talking to Jesus had the perfect profile of a Reed graduate.

These lawyers insisted on the primacy of learning. They delighted in any abstract discussion of the law. Ancient Galileans were constantly amazed that the Pharisees could spend hours discussing whether it was mint or rue that ought to be tithed. So along came an intellectual lawyer. He was theologically sophisticated and probably thought he would trap this rather naive carpenter into a great theological debate and dazzle him with his brilliance.

"How do you inherit eternal life?" counsel asked. He

probably had anticipated Jesus' every response, except the one he actually got. Jesus did the one thing he had not counted on. He did not give him an answer, but asked him a question instead (a model in evangelism we could well apply).

"What is written in the law. How do you read?" Jesus asked.

Counsel answered, "You shall love the Lord your God with all your heart, and with all your soul, and with all your strength, and with all your mind; and your neighbor as yourself."

"You have answered right; do this, and you will live," Jesus replied.

Counsel, becoming defensive, asked, "Who is my neighbor?"

And so Jesus told him the now familiar parable of the Good Samaritan. The dynamics in the story are fascinating.

Imagine the most brilliant person you know approaching Jesus rather smugly with an enormous theological question. Jesus responds with a question that forces him or her to recite an answer they learned as a child. It is like saying, "That's a very good question. Now can you remember what you learned in third grade?" They answer quickly, feeling somewhat embarrassed and defensive. Now can you think of anything much clearer than the statement, "Love your neighbor"? One would like to think a brilliant theologian might grasp its meaning.

What is this lawyer really reacting to? He wanted a nice, abstract religious discussion. He wanted to parade his knowledge before Jesus. But Jesus called him to act on what he knew. This is not an example of Jesus putting down intellectual thought. On the contrary, Jesus was a supreme intellectual here, for he knew that truth must be evidenced in one's life not put away in cold storage. But the lawyer felt how awkward and annoying! He wanted something sublime and esoteric—a rare pearl—not being told to love some bland and insignificant neighbor!

So when Jesus became specific (as he always does), the lawyer tried to find a way to crawl out. "Well, what does it really mean to love my neighbor? The whole thing is so complex," he retorted. "I don't want to rush into anything. What if I went out and loved someone and it turned out not to be my neighbor? I think we need to study this, have a conference on it."

Instead Jesus told the lawyer a story about "neighborliness" and asked him to identify the real neighbor. Then he concluded the conversation: "You go do the same and you will live."

Jesus summed up life here in terms of a love relationship to God, to our neighbor and to ourselves. Before any religious activity our lives are to bear the stamp of profound love. The priest in the parable of the Good Samaritan did not stop to help the victim, perhaps because he was on the way to temple. In other words, he thought more of religion than he did that man. His actions reflected his theology.

It is always that way. Our sociology reflects our theology. The way we treat others reveals what we think God is like. Imagine the implications this has for evangelism! The way we treat others is critical. People will understand as much of the love of God as they see in our own lives. The first Bible many people will read will be your life.

We are called, therefore, to mirror the love of God—a love that is so extravagant that we must never keep it to ourselves. We must spread it around. It is not a mushy love, all sentiment and no action. Jesus' love drove him deeply into the lives of people. He cared for their wholeness. When he went out into a day he did not ask himself, "Is this my social action day or do I give them the salvation message?" Jesus cared for people as he found them. So must we care for their wholeness —spiritual, social, psychological, you name it.

And how are we to love and be a neighbor to those whom we do not know (which constitutes the bulk of the world's population)? Reinhold Niebuhr once wrote, "Love must be aggressively translated into simple justice." My husband, Wes, has expanded this concept to mean that pursuing justice is one way we can love those persons we will never know—and that's 99.99 per cent of the world's population.[9] The call to a love relationship will involve much more than emotional empathy. It requires fighting against injustice. Again, our actions as Christians will reflect how just we believe God actually is.

Finally, Jesus' call to relationship involves the law. The Pharisees were correct in taking the law seriously. (Law in this sense means not only the Ten Commandments but the whole of God's moral law in the Old and New Testaments.) The irony is that they did not take the law seriously enough. We in the twentieth century tend to neglect God's law too much. But we must not abandon the law as having meaning only for the people of the Old Testament. The call to relationship and the call to honor God's laws actually go well together. Our love for God, others and ourselves, and all the actions that this relationship entails, mirrors what the law is all about and what it is preparing us for. We do not try to prove our own righteousness by obeying the law, as some of the Pharisees tried to do. Rather we accept the law's verdict on us: we are sinners.

Moreover, we acknowledge that only when we live "according to the Spirit" can we fulfill the law's righteous requirements. By living in Christ's Spirit we joyfully submit to God's law, because it tells us what is pleasing to God, what the things of the Spirit are and what it means practically to walk in the Spirit.

If the Pharisees had properly understood the whole of the law, they would have understood the call to relationship. In fact, one of the most well-known passages of Old Testament law highlights this: "Hear, O Israel: The LORD our God is one Lord; and you shall love the LORD your God with all your heart, and with all your soul, and with all your might"

(Deut. 6:4-5). Instead they denied their relationship as the young prodigal did to his father and, subsequently as the elder brother did to his younger prodigal brother. And consequently the Pharisees had no message to the lost.

People or Programs?

I remember being with a Christian student on a beach. Bob and I met several non-Christians and began talking about all sorts of things. Eventually the conversation got around to Christianity, and it was a lively and invigorating discussion. We even exchanged addresses before leaving. I was feeling very good about the conversation, but Bob seemed very quiet.

When I asked him what was wrong he said, "I thought it was an absolute failure. There are four major points to the gospel and you only brought in two of them, and they weren't even in the right order!"

I said, "What were the names of the three people we met this afternoon?"

"Oh, I don't know," he said. "What in the world difference does that make? There were two girls and one guy, or was it the other way around?"

I stared at him in disbelief and sadness. Here was a young man who genuinely loved God. He was exceedingly religious and sincere. I doubt that he ever missed a daily quiet time. And yet he had missed the entire point. He was sure his agenda, his four points, were the supreme value. Yet his program was so rigid that real live human beings could not penetrate it. We must beware of this kind of Pharisaism, for it is so frequently the disease of the devoted. This student was so busy rehearsing his four points of salvation that he forgot that he was speaking to the very people Christ had come to save.

We must never forget that to be a follower of Jesus is to be dominated by love. We may not be well versed in Scripture, or have a seminary background; we may be timid and unsure of ourselves. But we have arms and hearts that were meant to be used. We must ask ourselves, Do I treat people as royalty walking the earth? My parents, my spouse, my roommate, the student on the floor that I can't stand? Do I believe that by merely seeing me God would break into a run and embrace me? Does my life reflect only religious activity or does it bear the mark of profound love? When our lives are characterized by the love of Christ, we can begin to interest people in the gospel.

A Question of Holiness:
Jesus and the Pharisees

5

I WAS VISITING OREGON STATE University for several days
and was trying to get to know the nonbelievers who lived in the
dorm where I was staying. One night I learned there was an
excellent movie on television and, suspecting there would be a
large crowd, I went. The room was packed with students,
popcorn and Coke bottles. During commercials we laughed
and talked, and I answered why I was visiting their campus.
Friendships began to form between myself and several others.
A majority of those students came to hear me when I gave a
campus talk later that week.

While we were watching television, however, a Christian
girl walked by and looked at us a bit disapprovingly, then saw
me and left bewildered. Later she came to me and wondered
why I would do such a frivolous thing as watch TV, when it
wasn't even a Christian program. Didn't I feel it was wrong?
Shouldn't I have been upstairs praying for them and my talk
rather than living exactly as they did? Was I giving them a

worldly model instead of a spiritual one?

This incident raises some very important questions for us in evangelism. For example, what does it mean to be holy? How much are we to identify with the world? When are we in danger of being indistinguishable from the world? Many times I've seen Christians keep arms length from their non-Christian friends because they thought they were being spiritual. But when our understanding of spirituality isolates us from people as well as our culture, then we, like the Pharisees have misunderstood true holiness. If we grasp Jesus' approach to holiness, we will not be isolated from others but neither will we be identical. Another look at Jesus' conflict with the Pharisees will be helpful.

The Pharisees' Understanding of Holiness

Jesus and the Pharisees clashed violently over their understanding of holiness and how it should be demonstrated. The Pharisees believed Jesus was not a holy man for he violated their understanding of holiness which they drew largely from the Levitical laws of purity and the Tradition of the Elders. They knew God had called them to be a holy people—set apart. And they translated that almost exclusively in terms of separation and purification, even though maintaining holiness and piety came at a high price. In order to grasp the implications this has for evangelism we need to examine a few specific issues. Twelve treatises of the Mishna discuss the subject of purification. We will look at four.

First, the *Sabbath*. The Scriptures taught that we are to rest and not work on the Sabbath (Ex. 20:8-11). However, their rabbis defined what would be considered work. For example, the Pharisees were so afraid of working on the Sabbath that there was a law stating, "A fracture may not be attended to. If anyone has sprained his ankle or foot, he may not pour cold water on it."[1] Hillel later wrote, however, that one should indeed work on the Sabbath if a friend was at the point of death. The Pharisees, of course, were terribly upset by all of the activity that Jesus engaged in on the Sabbath.

Second, *handwashing*. The Pharisees were taught by their Tradition of the Elders that "he who lightly esteems hand-washing will perish from the earth."[2] This is why in Luke 11:37-38 a Pharisee dining with Jesus was so astonished that Jesus did not first wash his hands before dinner. A holy man would not have neglected that, as far as they were concerned.

Third, *no association with sinners*. The Pharisees were constantly astonished by the company Jesus kept. Jesus not only liked talking with sinners, he even ate dinner with them. The Pharisees on the other hand avoided or regulated the rest of the population by a system of elaborate precautions designed to minimize ritual uncleanness. They would not entertain guests other than those who attempted to keep the law (Jesus perhaps was an exception).

Fourth, *clean and unclean food and animals*. The rabbis found 49 reasons for declaring animals clean or unclean. They pronounced 700 kinds of fish and 24 kinds of birds unclean.[3] The book of Numbers (chapters 13 and 14) already explained what was unclean, such as the human corpse, but "the Pharisaic teacher defined the minimum size of the corpse's parts which can cause defilement upon contact, e.g., a bone as large as a barley corn."[4]

There were uncounted other laws. But from these we can see that holy behavior was to be determined through obedience to ceremonial laws. We must remember that Jesus did not criticize the Pharisees for maintaining the Levitical laws, but for ignoring other aspects of holiness that he said were more significant. Our view of holiness is generally traceable to our view of human corruption. What, then, was the Pharisees' understanding of evil? They seem to have ignored the inner aspect of both evil and righteousness. For example, Jesus charged them, "Now you Pharisees cleanse the outside of the cup and of the dish, but inside you are full of extortion and wickedness" (Lk. 11:39). Again, he said to them, "You tithe mint and dill and cummin, and have neglected the weightier matters of the law, justice and mercy and faith" (Mt. 23:23). And again, "You blind guides, straining out a gnat and swallowing a camel" (Mt. 23:24). Matthew 23 and Luke 11:37—12:12 contain many such accusations.

The general tenor of these remarks could cause us to infer that to the Pharisees evil was essentially external in nature, and not deriving from within as Jesus suggests. But we cannot conclude this. If Jesus criticized them so severely for ignoring the internal aspects of sin, it implies that they knew better. He held them accountable to a truth they knew but were not practicing. Why should they have known better?

First, the Old Testament is a profoundly moral book. Through Moses came the first major expression of the depths of God's concern for morality, for instance, in the Ten Commandments. Nathan boldly rebuked David concerning moral fault with Bathsheba (2 Sam. 12:1-9) and Elijah confronted Ahab concerning Naboth's vineyard (1 Kings 21:17-19). But the moral nature of God is chiefly brought home to us through the prophets Amos, Hosea and Isaiah. The Old Testament indeed dealt seriously with the question of inner sin and morality.

Second, it is a common misconception that the law only referred to external conformity and not a conformity of the heart. The facts are otherwise. As Oehler says, "The law insists on the disposition of the heart, when it says in Exodus 20:17, 'Thou shalt not covet'; when it binds men to love God with the whole heart and soul, to be placable toward their fellow men, and the like, Deut. 6:5; Lev. 19:17."[5] H. W. Robinson adds a similar note, "Even the Priestly Code, with all its elaborate precautions for ceremonial holiness, is still in large measure, a moral document, the outcome of a passion for perfection that shall be worthy of Yahweh."[6]

Finally, the holiness code in Leviticus begins in chapter 19 with, "You shall be holy; for I the LORD your God am holy" (v. 2). Then toward the end of chapter 20 the Lord says again, "You shall be holy to me; for I the LORD am holy" (v. 26).

It's as if these two declarations were parentheses, and everything inside them had to do with what it meant to be holy. And what do Leviticus 19 and 20 say about being holy? Revere your parents. Do not steal or lie. Be a good neighbor. Be reasonable with your neighbor. Pay a decent wage. Do no injustice. Be not partial to the poor or defer to the great. Give honest weights and measures. A remarkable recitation of what it means to be holy. We may think of God's holiness as only in the heavens. But God sees holiness lived out on the roads and streets of our daily lives. We may think of God's holiness as separation. But God sees his holiness lived out in our relationships. We may think of God's holiness in his deity, but God sees holiness lived out in the way we treat other people.[7]

Why the Pharisees focused so exclusively on the ceremonial law when they had such vast riches of moral literature to draw upon is not fully known. What we do know is that Jesus held them accountable for the whole of Scripture—and legitimately so.

The upshot is that the critics of Jesus concerned themselves with the external ceremonial manifestations of sin. Even though their teaching showed otherwise, they behaved as if evil came only from the outside. When one's concern is only for external evil, then the logical way to avoid being "contaminated" is to avoid the object altogether, or worse, to blame the object for causing the problem.

Take the problem of lust. Both Jesus and the Pharisees agreed it was wrong. But if one sees evil as externally imposed, then the culprit is not one's desire but the person desired. One very orthodox sect called the "Bruised and Bleeding" Pharisees thought lust was evil. So they determined they would avoid the source of the problem—namely, women.

And whenever they came into the presence of a woman, not only would they avoid talking to her, they would close their eyes so they could not see her at all. Of course this caused them to run into walls, and hence their name. Can you imagine the shock of an exceedingly pious member of the "Bruised and Bleeding" sect walking by and discovering Jesus deeply engaged in conversation with a prostitute? Activity like this made it difficult for them to believe that Jesus was a holy man.

And so the Pharisees failed to see the devastating power and effect of such internal sins as pride, jealousy and uncharitableness.

Jesus' Understanding of Holiness

Both Jesus and the Pharisees agreed that being holy was of fundamental importance. They agreed that God's historical purpose was to call out a people for himself; that this people would be a holy people, set apart from the world to belong to him and to obey him; and that their holiness or difference would be seen in all their behavior and outlook. Jesus demonstrated in his Sermon on the Mount how clearly he believed that we were to be different. In Matthew 6:8 he said, "Do not be like them." Our character is to be completely distinct from what the world celebrates.

Jesus required a righteousness to exceed even that of the scribes and Pharisees, and to be demonstrated in the totality of his followers' lives—both in ethical behavior and religious devotion. Jesus took holiness seriously, but he and the Pharisees radically differed over the nature of holiness. Let us look at four examples, the first three of which parallel those we examined above.

First, the *Sabbath*. The Pharisees moaned over Jesus' abuse of the Sabbath. Why wouldn't he heal Monday-Wednesday-Friday? Even a Tuesday-Thursday routine would have been fine. Why did he have to pick the Sabbath? They felt his healing on the Sabbath constituted work. Jesus said their interpretation was wrong: "The sabbath was made for man, not man for the sabbath" (Mk. 2:27). Jesus was not saying that rest on the Sabbath was unimportant. But the Pharisees said they wanted to live according to God's laws; so, ironically, while they carefully avoided working on the Sabbath, they plotted to kill Jesus.

Second, *handwashing*. When Jesus did not wash his hands before eating, it offended the Pharisees. Jesus told them that their emphasis was on the wrong thing: "You Pharisees cleanse the outside of the cup and of the dish but inside you are full of extortion and wickedness. You fools! Did not he who made the outside make the inside also?" (Lk. 11: 39-40). Jesus required heart righteousness rather than mere rule righteousness.

Third, *association with sinners*. While the Pharisees despised sinners, Jesus loved them. The Pharisees as well as his disciples wanted to avoid any contact, but Jesus sought them out. The Pharisees thought association with a "sinner" would contaminate them. Jesus said the source of sin came from within. And the holiness of Jesus, far from isolating him from people, drove him into troubled lives. Instead of making him walk away from people, it made him welcome them.

Fourth, *piety*. Jesus agreed with the Pharisees that piety is important. But the motive for tithing, praying and fasting must be to glorify God not themselves as the Pharisees tended to do (Mt. 6:1-8). Jesus warned against "practicing your piety before men in order to be seen by them" (v. 1), and he said that we must not focus on the external and neglect the more important internal aspects of piety. Concerning tithing, for example, Jesus told them, "Woe to you Pharisees! for you tithe mint and rue and every herb, and neglect justice and the love of God; these you ought to have done, without neglecting the others" (Lk. 11:42). He tells them not that they are wrong to tithe—but that they have neglected other areas of vital importance.

Radical Identification, Radical Difference
The Pharisees understood holiness in terms of ceremonial
purification and separation from the masses. But Jesus
demonstrated what holiness is through his radical identification and his radical difference from the world. As Robertson
comments, the Pharisees "were aloof in spirit and built up a
hedge around themselves to keep off infection. Jesus plunged
into the midst of the disease and sin to root both out."[8] Jesus
walked alongside of people. He was approachable. He
allowed a prostitute at Simon's banquet to express her love
and devotion to him by touching him (Lk. 7:36-50). He accepted people as they were.

But we must remember the other side too. Jesus called his
disciples to be different as well. He identified, yes, but he was
never identical to the world. My fear today is that we may
enjoy talking of the Christian's pharisaic problem while we
ignore the call to be different. We must never try to escape
from the truth that there is a fundamental difference between
Christians and non-Christians. If we ignore or minimize this
difference, we will be of little use to God or to the world.

Jesus tells us that we are salt and light (Mt. 5:13-16). Jesus
does not say that we are to become light. Jesus says, "You are
light." So we must begin reflecting who we really are and not
try to hide it.

Perhaps our mistake is to settle for a far too superficial difference, one that focuses mostly on externals and personal
disciplines. If you asked non-Christians what they felt made a
Christian different their answer probably would be frightfully
inadequate. Recently in an evangelistic talk I asked the non-
Christians what they thought the big issues were for
Christians, what we truly fight for.

In utter seriousness a boy answered, "Judging from what
I've seen, you stand against swearing, dirty jokes and rowdy
parties. Isn't that right?"

"I think there are larger issues than that for Christians," I said. "For example, I'm against murder."

Everyone laughed, and he said, "I hardly think anyone wouldn't be, but that issue doesn't come up very often."

"Oh? Do you know how Jesus defines murder? He says it's murder when we destroy people with our words. It's murder when we put people down and treat them as insignificant. If I saw that happening, which I do frequently, as a Christian I would have to stand against it." I was referring here to Jesus' Sermon on the Mount, especially Matthew 5:21-22.

There was an instant hush in the audience. He said, "I had no idea that Christianity had anything to do with how you treat people. I thought it was merely do's and don'ts."

How then are we to be different? John Stott in his treatment of the Sermon on the Mount summarizes this portion of Matthew, and consequently defines our "difference" this way: (1) A Christian's character (for example, we thirst for righteousness, we are peacemakers, we are pure in heart); (2) a Christian's influence (we are salt and light in our communities); (3) a Christian's righteousness (we are conformed to God's moral teaching); (4) a Christian's piety (which is marked by our sincerity of devotion); (5) a Christian's ambitions (we seek first the glory of God instead of self-centered material wealth and possession); (6) a Christian's relationships (we do not judge others but we serve them, etc.); and (7) a Christian's commitment (we obey Christ as Lord).[9]

I frequently hear that the call to be holy and the call to demonstrate love to sinners are mutually exclusive. (As if love is the antithesis to holiness!) Jesus welcomed and loved sinners; he did not drive them away by too much affectation of righteousness. He showed genuine compassion for people, but he was also direct and uncompromising in denouncing sin. Jesus had compassion, but there was also toughness in his love. He won them without sacrificing the purity of his life.

The paradox of agape love is that we accept our neighbor unconditionally and with open arms and at the same time

desire moral purity for their lives. If Jesus is our Lord, our
compassion will be shaped by his moral absolutes. Christ both
was merciful and made judgments. Some things, he said, were
immoral and destructive, but he never ceased to love. Indeed,
it was his love that prompted his judgment. The enemy of our
age is our desire to be tolerant and open-minded. But the
problem with being too open-minded is that our brains fall
out.

I know a Christian woman who has cared deeply for a non-
Christian woman who has had every variety of sexual experience. One day the non-Christian woman said to the Christian, "It's funny, my non-Christian friends accept me. They
say it doesn't matter what I do. I'm free. But it's only with you
that I feel loved, that I know I could always come to you. But
it's also only when I'm with you that I feel shame and remorse
for what I'm doing."

That is holiness. It never abandons; it identifies deeply with
individual people. But it also brings the reality of God's presence, the purity of his holiness. It is not intimidated by nor
does it flee from crisis; neither does it deny the reality of existence.

So we must ask ourselves, Do I identify enough? Do I wel-
come people? Or am I a member of the Holy Huddle, the local
God Squad? Do I hang around people of various beliefs and
mores? Do I love the unlovely? Or, on the other hand, am I
different enough? Am I Christlike? Do I bring this aspect of
Christ's holiness, of his moral standards, of the fruit of the
Spirit? Or out of my sincere desire to identify and to love, have
I become culture accommodating?

Dr. Edward Bauman, minister of Foundry United Metho-
dist Church in Washington, D.C. (and my own pastor), said in
a sermon that Jesus had the ministry of the towel but he also
had the ministry of the whip. Our lives as Christians, if we are
to be effective evangelists, should reflect that same dual
stance toward the world.

A Question of Obedience: Jesus and the Pharisees

6

WHEN WE LISTEN TO SOMEONE explain how we get to know God, we hear frequent references to believing on Jesus, opening up our hearts to him or asking him to come into our lives. We are to make a decision for Christ or pray a prayer or walk down an aisle. Of course, these things—believing, deciding, accepting—really are essential.

But how often do we hear references to a genuine change in the direction of our lives? How often do we ourselves, as we tell someone about Jesus, point out that obedience to Christ as Lord is also involved? Cathy, for instance, could have avoided making fundamental mistakes if she had understood the importance of obedience.

The Pharisees' View of Knowing God

The Pharisees studied God. They memorized the Scriptures and knew every word. They devised games with their scrolls. They would throw a dart into a rolled-up scroll. The word would be read where the dart landed and they would then have to recite the rest of the verse. They felt that through study they could find God and that knowledge was the avenue to transformation. Jesus himself commented to the Pharisees, "You search the scriptures, because you think that in them you have eternal life" (Jn. 5:39). To know the Scriptures is to know God, they thought.

There are two points to be made about the Pharisees in this regard. First, knowledge is not enough for salvation. The Pharisees considered themselves supremely righteous because of their vast knowledge. But they misunderstood a vital point. Mere information makes no one righteous; it only makes us responsible for what we know. It is impotent to effect lasting and real change within us. One may be overeducated and untransformed.

The Hebrews' understanding of knowledge, however, is that the degree to which we know something is the degree to which we have integrated it into our life. It is of no use to say we believe in something when our actions betray our beliefs. To know is not only to verbalize; it is to act as well. The Pharisees are a positive model for us. They knew that if they spoke of faith in God, there must be evidence or fruit in their lives to demonstrate this faith.

So the Pharisees took obedience seriously. They tried tediously to obey the ceremonial laws. In fact they could hardly obey enough. They constantly kept adding new laws. But they understood one very important thing: we are responsible for what we know. Knowledge must automatically translate into obedience, be it words or action. And so the Pharisees tried to integrate into their lives merely the part of Scripture they chose to focus upon.

So the key question is, What does it mean to obey? We must learn from the Pharisees' mistakes here. There are three basic issues. The first issue is: *what* do we obey? Jesus told them they sought life in the wrong place. He said life was found in himself. The Scriptures pointed to him, but they were not to be worshiped.

Jesus also pointed out the irony that the Pharisees claimed to revere Scripture yet they rejected the very person that Scripture proclaimed. If they really believed Scripture, they would have believed in Jesus and they would have been drawn to worship him. So an attempt merely to obey the laws of the Bible is not enough. We must obey Christ. Indeed, it is our failure to obey God's law that drives us to realize that we need the inner transformation that Christ offers.

The second issue is: *why* must we obey? The motive for our obedience is as important as the act of obedience itself. God requires heart obedience that is motivated by our love and sincerity of devotion to him. Merely to obey rules at a superficial level and not to allow God total access to our person prevents us from having deep contact with God. We do not obey in order to earn our salvation. We must not obey out of pride. Rather we obey because of who God is and the marvelous work he has done in seeking and saving us. It was something we could never have done on our own.

The third issue is: *how broad* is the scope of our obedience? The answer is absolute and universal. We are called to obey the *whole* revelation of God. We must not pick and choose what we obey as the Pharisees did. We cannot focus on the aspects of Scripture we find appealing and ignore that which is hard or uncomfortable.

It is true, of course, that none of us can encompass the depth of all God's desires for us as expressed in Scripture. We are finite. But what we know we must obey. We are called on to meditate on his Word consciously and regularly, to ignore no portion of it by design or planned blindness, to read both Old and New Testaments, both the law and the prophets, both the Gospels and Epistles. It is only by such a sweep that we can help prevent the sort of blindness evidenced by the Pharisees.

Jesus' View of Knowing God

How do we find God and grow in him? Jesus was adamant at
this point. He said we must do what he says. We must put into
practical obedience the knowledge that we have. He continually asked people to drop their nets, to sell all they had and
to follow him.

We might say that Jesus had a theology of obedience. And
the object of this obedience was a living person, not a historical
norm, not a code of laws, but himself. He called people to be
accountable to God whether they were believers or skeptics
who were searching. For example, he told his disciples, "What
is the point of calling me, 'Lord, Lord,' without doing what I
tell you to do?" (Lk. 6:46 Phillips).

To the Pharisaic lawyer who came to trap him in debate,
Jesus' response was no different (Lk. 10:25-37). "How do you
inherit eternal life," the lawyer asked. And Jesus told him to
recite what he understood, which was to love God totally as
well as his neighbors as himself.

This lawyer was not a follower of Jesus, and his motive in
the conversation was "to put him to the test" (v. 25). So how
did Jesus help him understand the true way? Well, by many
standards of evangelizing Jesus did a rotten job. Jesus did not
have the lawyer "pray the prayer." Nor did Jesus ask him to
read a tract on the five points that lead to salvation, nor was he
asked to kindly recite the five points of Calvinism. He simply
said, "Go and do it." In other words, "Begin to put into practical obedience what you understand." He called him to be responsible to the light he had already received.

Jesus knew that obedience to his and his Father's words
yielded faith; that revelation is based upon obedience. Over
and over again Jesus in the Gospels called people to faith and
obedience. If I had to sum up one's response to the gospel
message, I would say as William Pannell has said, "It's paint—
or get off the ladder." Jesus approached people exactly like
that. He told them to pick up their brush and paint something.

Do you want to discover who Jesus is and deal honestly with your doubts? Jesus' style is not to suggest that you go and ponder the virgin birth for three months but to begin doing what he says. This challenge can mean much to us as we engage in evangelism.

Jesus' emphasis on obedience is greatly needed today. Unfortunately much of Western theology is overintellectualized. Biblical theology, on the other hand, is intimately connected with action and life; it is associated with the situation we live in. One of the most helpful aspects of the liberation theology has been its biblical emphasis on the importance of practice. If the Pharisees thought that through knowledge and legalistic obedience one could know God, our present generation may be in even worse shape. We tend to think of knowledge only in cerebral terms.

Whenever I ask students if they learned much at a weekend conference, they often answer, "Oh, yeah. You should see how many notebooks I filled."

And my response is, "You don't have to show me your notebooks. If you learned anything, I'll see it in your life."

Jesus was not the originator of the call to obedience. In the Old Testament as well as the New there is a consensus. Indeed Yahweh's purpose is that we should learn to say, "I delight to do thy will, O my God" (Ps. 40:8). God seeks our fellowship with him through our moral obedience. H. W. Robinson writes, "This is salvation in the deeper and more spiritual sense of the Old Testament. . . . But even in the religion of the Law, . . . *obedience* to the revealed will of Yahweh is recognized as the supreme end of man and the supreme glory of God. The attitude of Jesus to the will of God and his emphasis on the absolute worth of obedience as the supreme 'value' of human life are the best illustrations of what the Old Testament indicates as the purposes of Yahweh in creation and providence."[1] Obedience is critical because it reveals a harmony of purpose between the human will and the divine.

And Jesus is our supreme example of one who was utterly obedient to the Father's will.

Jesus' emphasis on faith and obedience also helps us understand the role of repentance in conversion and discipleship. Too many people believe a Christian is a person who has simply "prayed the prayer" and "decided" for Jesus. But many such "Christians" do not live as if they are under new management. They may claim that they once made a decision, but everything else in their life is unchanged. What a superficial understanding of what it means to be a Christian!

Too many people have stopped at the door that leads to conversion. The door (be it a prayer, a decision or whatever) is simply that—a door. It was closed and it has been opened for one express purpose: so we can go through it and get involved in life on the other side. But some see conversion and discipleship as a revolving door that will allow them to stay there without ever actually participating in life on the other side. They have come to glorify their experience of the door when it was meant only as an avenue of passage to a new life. In fact, it is not our "door experience" but our new life that demonstrates whether we have been converted.

A true disciple of Jesus is one who does what Jesus does—obeys the will of God. When Jesus called people to obedience, he was calling them to be accountable to God, to begin living for him as he desires. "To convert means far more than to experience the psychological, emotional aspects of change through an inner experience," writes Jim Wallis. "The biblical accent is clearly on a reversal of direction, a transfer of loyalties, a change in commitment leading to the creation of a new community. . . . It is a radical change in the whole of one's life and in all of one's relationships to the world. . . . We have forgotten that a relationship to Christ means a relationship to the purposes of Christ in history."[2]

Why did Jesus call even those who were not following him to obedience? Perhaps so that their experience of conversion (that is, one of obedience) would teach them what it means to be a disciple. The more I read the Gospels the more I realize how vital it is for skeptics to understand this. Frequently I meet non-Christians who are not ready to pray and ask Christ to be the Lord of their lives. What are we to say to those who want to know if Jesus is the way but still need to "check Jesus out" before they are guided by the Spirit into conversion?

Based on my understanding of the gospel (and the insight of Gene Thomas) I now say to nonbelievers, "Tell God (or the four walls if that is the one you think you are speaking to) that you want to find out if Jesus is truly God. And that if you could feel more certain you would follow him. Then begin to read the Gospels, every day. Each day as you read, something will probably hit you and make sense. Whatever that is, do it as soon as you can." In other words, I call them to act on whatever strikes them as true and to do it if they are sincerely seeking God (and not trying to earn salvation by works of righteousness).

The Battle of the Desk

One day Sue, a very bright student, came to me. She told me she was an agnostic but that her best friend, Larry, had become a Christian. He talked to her a lot about his faith and did not neglect her after his conversion. Instead he brought her to his campus Christian gatherings and introduced her to his new Christian friends. He made her feel comfortable and a part of his very different Christian world. He answered as best he could her many intellectual questions about his faith. And most importantly, he loved her.

"I've seen what Christ has done for Larry," she told me. "I see the love these Christians have for each other and for me. I've seen what Jesus is like in the Gospels and a lot of my questions have been answered. But I still don't believe. I'd like to find God. But I'm plagued with doubts. Please don't ask me to pray to receive Christ; it'd be dishonest. What should I do?"

I suggested what I mentioned above. She gulped and said, "That's radical. But I'll do it."

So she began having what she called her "pagan quiet times." And the Christians around her prayed that God would speak to her in the Scriptures and give her concrete situations in which she could obey. Several months later she said she wanted to talk to me. Here is Sue's story:

"One day I read in the Bible, 'If someone steals your coat, don't let him have only that, but offer your cloak as well.' For whatever reason, that verse hit me between the eyes. So I said to the four walls, 'Listen, walls—or God if you're there—I'm going to do what this verse says, if the opportunity arises today. I want to remind you that I'm trying to do things your way in order to find out if you exist and if Jesus really is who he says. Amen.'

"The day went by and I forgot the verse. Then I headed to the library to continue working on my senior thesis. Just as I sat down at my designated thesis desk this guy comes up and starts yelling at me. He told me the school hadn't given him his thesis desk so he was going to take mine. (Everyone knows how important your thesis desk is for your work. The school only gives you one.) I started yelling back and pretty soon we caused quite a ruckus. But it was when he glared at me and said, 'Look. I'm stealing it from you whether you like it or not' that it suddenly hit me.

"I just looked at him and moaned, 'OHHHHH, no. No. I can't believe it.' And to myself I thought, 'Look, God, if you're there, I do want to know if Jesus is God. But isn't there some other way of finding out besides obeying that verse? I mean, couldn't I tithe or get baptized or give up something else? But DON'T TAKE MY THESIS DESK! I mean with my luck, I'll give up the desk and then discover that you don't exist.'

"But I couldn't escape the fact that I had read that verse the very same day someone tried to rob me. Before, I had always been amused to see how Jesus aimed for the jugular vein in his conversations with people in the Bible. But now it didn't feel so funny. I took a deep breath, tried not to swear and said, 'OK, you can have the desk.'

"He looked bewildered. But just at that moment the librarian came up. She said she'd heard the conversation and was outraged. Then the boy began swearing at her and intimidated her so much that she told us we had to see his thesis advisor. So the three of us trotted over to his advisor's office. The more the boy swore the more nervous the advisor became. He told us he couldn't make the final decision but we should go to the head of the department. The head of the department told us exactly the same thing but urged us to see the dean of men. And the dean of men guided us to someone else. And finally the last person we saw said, 'Well, what does Sue think we should do?'

"All this time I kept thinking about what I'd seen in these past several months. I'd seen Larry's life changed. I'd seen something beautiful in this Christian fellowship, something so real I could almost touch it. Even though I was not a Christian, I had been loved by these people. And I'd seen Jesus in the Bible. I felt so drawn to him. I realized, even without a thesis desk, somehow I still had more than this poor pathetic boy. I told them he could have the desk and the meeting was over.

"But when we walked out the door this guy grabbed my arm and asked me why in the world I let him have it. I told him he would think I'd really flipped out, but I was trying to discover if Jesus was really who he claimed to be. I was attempting to do the things he told us to do. 'I've been reading what he says in the Gospels. And today I read that if somebody tried to rip me off I was supposed to let them and even throw in something extra to boot.' All I could see were the whites of his eyes. 'So I'm going to give you the desk but don't press your luck about something extra.'

"Then he asked, 'Why in the world would Jesus say such a crazy thing?'

"Then I said, 'Hey, if there's one thing I've learned from reading about Jesus and meeting some real Christians, it's that Jesus would give you a whole lot more than a thesis desk if you'd let him. I know Jesus would give it to you. So that thesis desk is yours.'

"As I said those words, I just simply *knew* it was all true. I kinda felt like God was saying, 'Well done. That's the way I want my children to behave.' "

There were a lot of things that Sue did not understand about being a Christian when she became one. But there was one thing she did know. To follow Jesus is to do what he says. I am not suggesting that we must do this with every skeptic we meet. But this understanding of obedience must permeate more of our evangelism. Obviously we must be sensitive to what the Holy Spirit is doing in a person's life. But we need to call people to as much commitment as they have been prepared for.

Not everyone we meet is ready to accept Christ as Savior. But everyone is on a continuum in their relationship to Christ. Our task is to draw them closer to the point where they choose to become disciples. One way to do this is to call them to accountability for what they know. We do not need to be belligerent. A gentle suggestion can be devastatingly effective.

The Call to Repentance

Jesus calls skeptics to obedience for another reason. The call to obey can also be a call to repentance. Jesus told the lawyer in Luke 10:37 to go be a "neighbor" like the Good Samaritan. Superficially that sounds like sheer humanism. Jesus seemingly forgot to tell the lawyer he was the Son of God, that salvation rests in him alone, indeed that it is only through Jesus that we can truly love our neighbor anyway! But maybe Jesus had a different strategy. Jesus called him to obey the light he had been given.

Suppose the lawyer went out and sincerely tried to love his

neighbor in ways he had never tried before. And since his consciousness had been raised, he would be more sensitive to failure than ever before. Suppose he realized he could not cut the mustard. The harder he tried to love the more he was aware of his inadequacies. Perhaps on a return visit to Jesus he would say, "I need help. I can't do it. I tried to do what you said. Where do I go to get help?" I have a hunch Jesus' second conversation would be very different from the first.

To encourage people to reach out to God, to put him to the test, to do what he says (as a means of finding out if God is there) is to communicate that God is alive. We must live by our belief that the kingdom of God is at hand. We believe God is living and at work. Our faith is not in a historical model. It is in a living Lord. This sense of the aliveness and nearness of God must permeate our evangelism. As Chesterton writes, "Plato has told you a truth; but Plato is dead. Shakespeare has startled you with an image; but Shakespeare will not startle you any more. But imagine what it would be to live with such men still living, to know that Plato might break out with an original lecture tomorrow, or that at any moment Shakespeare might shatter everything with a simple song." The person who lives in contact with the living God is a person "always expecting to meet Plato or Shakespeare tomorrow at breakfast."[3]

Our evangelism will be more vital and substantial and our efforts long lasting when we help non-Christians see that God is alive and present, that they may discover him by putting his commands into practice and that real conviction that Jesus is God is evidenced not by sentimental feelings about God but by obedience to him. Indeed, it is through obedience that we discover who God is as well as deepen our knowledge of him.

A Lifestyle of Evangelism
In this and the previous two chapters we have looked at Jesus' lifestyle and priorities as demonstrated by his values in three

areas. We saw, first, that his life was marked by a deep love for God, his neighbor and himself. Then we noted how his holiness was reflected through his radical identification with the world as well as his radical difference from the world. Finally, we saw how his love and devotion to the Father were evidenced by his obedience to the Father's will.

If we are to be followers of Jesus, his values must permeate our values. We need to be concerned more with how our lives reflect his love, his holiness, his obedience, than with the latest witnessing techniques. When we live as Jesus did, in his power and with his presence, seekers will be drawn to us. Evangelism will not be a dreaded task to be ticked off every Wednesday. Rather, sharing Jesus will become a true delight and evangelism will become a lifestyle.

Christ with Us

7

IT IS EASY ENOUGH TO SAY THAT when we live our lives by Jesus' values evangelism will come naturally. But how do we live our lives like Jesus? It seems too much to ask. Jesus, after all, was God incarnate. I am just a human being—frail, frightened and essentially unable to live up to this ideal.

Of course, you alone can't live up to the ideal. Neither can I. But God knows this, and he has not left us to go it alone. Jesus is with us and by the power of the Holy Spirit he calls, equips and motivates us for ministry. This is the first bit of good news. The second is like it. The presence of Christ brings us his power and ability to use our limited resources in his limitless ways.

Third, Jesus is with us, not only by being in us through the indwelling of the Holy Spirit, but by being a part of those to whom we are called to minister. All people have been created in God's image. When we meet them in real personal encounter, we are meeting something of Christ. We are indeed not alone. And that's what we want to see more clearly now.

Jesus in Us

We may recall that Jesus told the Pharisee lawyer to be "a neighbor"! So is that all there is to being a disciple of Jesus? Is it merely to be kind and loving to the people next door? Is it simply to begin serving others? Luke apparently did not think so. For he followed this story with the familiar Mary and Martha passage (Lk. 10:38-42).

Immediately after Jesus told the lawyer to go and serve others we find Martha doing exactly what Jesus requested She was serving others by preparing a meal. But, we are told, she was "distracted with much serving." Why was this? Was she not doing all that Jesus required? Why couldn't she serve with peace and joy? Perhaps because she failed to do what Mary did. Mary allowed Jesus to serve *her* first. And Jesus said Mary had made a better choice.

This passage emphasizes that serving others is not enough. Indeed our ministry to others is dependent on our being fed by Christ himself. And it is the Holy Spirit who makes Jesus alive to us and nourishes him in us. Therefore, the Spirit of God is an absolute requisite for what we are called to do. We can learn all sorts of counseling skills, acquire techniques, develop razor-sharp programs in evangelism, but we will have no lasting impact unless God's Spirit is central in our ministry. We must ask for God's Spirit to anoint us and equip us for the ministry he calls us to. We can no more make a person become a Christian than we can make ourselves new people.

That is the frustration of the law. It can show us what to do, but it cannot make us want to do it. Only the Holy Spirit (and our obedient will) can bring about transformation. We must pray first for a renewal of the Holy Spirit in our lives as we seek to minister and then for his activity in the lives of the peo-

ple we are seeking. And in a mysterious way, prayer frees
God's Spirit to move.

Indeed, prayer is another absolute requisite for evangelizing, for through prayer God changes us and our friends into
the likeness of Christ. Just as we pray daily that God's Spirit
will renew us and equip us for the ministry he has called us to,
so must we pray daily for the conversion of our friends. And
not only for the long-range goal of conversion but the step-by-
step process of gradual acceptance that will result in conversion.

It is helpful to have a prayer partner, perhaps one other
Christian on your dorm floor or in your neighborhood who
wants to love that community through you. We need to be
diligent and persistent in praying for those God brings to us.

When I was in Spain and knew I would be studying at the
University of Illinois in the fall, I asked God to bring the most
open non-Christians and seat them next to me. For three
months in Spain I prayed for those whom God would put to
my right or my left in class.

When I arrived home, I called Beth Goldhor, a good friend,
and asked her if she would pray with me. We dreamed together, prayed together and set goals together. One goal was
that after the first month of school we would begin an evangelistic Bible study. One month later we started a study for our
non-Christian friends. Four of the ones I brought had sat next
to me the first day of class. Beth brought those she befriended
on her dorm floor the first week.

Ask God to show you just one or two people whom he wants
to seek through you. Find someone who will pray and share
that dream with you as Beth did with me. And remember in all
of this prayer and activity that great mystery of the indwelling
of Jesus—"Christ in you, the hope of glory" (Col. 1:27).

Jesus with Us
When we begin to realize the reality and power of Jesus' pres-

ence in our daily living, our evangelism takes on fresh force. The failure to see how dramatically Jesus' presence affects a situation is, however, a problem his followers have always had.

In Mark 6:30-44 the disciples had just returned from a successful preaching and healing journey. They were tired and Jesus suggested they go away in the boat to find a place to rest. But as they started to dock, they saw five thousand people waiting on shore for Jesus. (I am not so sure the disciples gave the crowd a big smile on first glimpse of them!) Jesus felt compassion for them since they looked like "sheep without a shepherd." So he taught them all day. When it grew dark and dinner time came, the disciples told Jesus to send the crowd away. When Jesus asked why they could not feed them, they responded cynically, "Oh, sure, with the thousand dollars we just happened to bring along?" But Jesus told them to divide the multitude into groups of hundreds and fifties. He took five loaves and two fish and thanked God for them. (No doubt Jesus was the only one who was grateful for so small an amount!) He touched the food and fed the five thousand.

How did the disciples fail here, and what can we learn from it? First, they failed to offer their limited resources. They looked at the task and their meager supplies and concluded it was impossible. They forgot that Jesus could take natural elements and do supernatural things with them.

Jesus did not look at the five loaves and two fish and say, "This is terrible. Such a tiny amount of food for all these people! I'll just have to do a miracle and whip up some food from nothing." It is significant that he worked with what the disciples had.

When we find ourselves in situations that seem beyond our limits (actually we should look for such situations!), we must not hesitate because we feel inadequate. We must not complain about our limited resources. God tells us he is glorified in our weakness. God's Spirit will take and multiply what we have.

Second, the disciples failed to see the power of Jesus' presence. Jesus prayed, touched the food and there was more than enough for everyone. Because of who he is, when Jesus touches anything, there is blessing.

But what about us? When we follow Jesus, his Spirit abides in us. That means he is a part of what we do. Everything we touch Jesus touches. If he touched the fish and multiplied them, then how does he touch our activities? He is with us when we gather for Bible study, when we eat and dance and work. And Jesus reaches out and touches others through us.

Maggie, a girl at the University of Oregon, was struck by Jesus' feeding the multitudes. She decided to reach out to her dorm floor by having an ice-cream party. She bought the ice cream, borrowed a scooper and said, "God, I have trouble believing that you can work through this ice-cream party to tell others of your love. But you dwell in me, so this isn't an ordinary ice-cream party. You are here. Love these people tonight."

I went to the party and the room was packed with hungry students. The atmosphere was lively and fun. To my knowledge no one had a spiritual discussion. Afterward she told me, "Well, it was a failure. I don't think Jesus was working here."

"Why?" I asked.

"Because no one even talked about him. All we did was have fun!"

Maggie demonstrated several misconceptions. First, that having fun was a waste of time. She felt every minute had to be used in serious spiritual pursuit. She did not feel God would approve of lively spontaneity. Second, she believed spiritual ministry only occurred when one was speaking about God. If that is true, then God has to work with severe limits. But it is not true. God works as powerfully through the nonverbal as he does through the verbal. We too must offer both. We need to let Jesus loose! Remember that Jesus is reaching out to everyone you are meeting. He wants to speak through everything that you do, not just your verbal witness.

The sequel to the ice-cream party shows this. Maggie told me the next day that eight students came to her. One girl said, "I couldn't believe you spent your money so we could eat! It was so much fun. You made our floor feel like a family for the first time. Why'd you do it?"

Another said, "My roommate and I had a great time. We decided we're going to have a party next week!"

And another, "It was so nice of you to do that. You know, I felt love bouncing off those walls. What are you into?"

Then Maggie said to me, "I told you Jesus wasn't at work at that party—that he wasn't showing people who he was. I am the Christian and never noticed him there, but my non-Christian friends did. They don't know who he is yet, but they sensed his presence. I wonder how much I've been limiting Jesus all along?"

When, through the power of the Holy Spirit, we let Jesus reach our dorm floor or neighborhood, he will create a family atmosphere. Jesus will give people a sense of worth. And his love is contagious; people will imitate it. They will be drawn to us at first without knowing why. What we must not forget is that we incarnate Jesus! Whatever our life intersects with, so does Jesus. Whomever we touch Jesus touches. We do not simply give the gospel, we are the gospel.

Jesus in Others

We know we are called to reach out and care for people. But some of us perhaps feel so painfully shy that we die a slow death in starting a conversation. Some of us do not feel naturally drawn to people. Reaching out to them seems foreign and makes us uncomfortable.

Learning to care for others requires several things. First, it demands practice. The disciples developed compassion very slowly. For most of them it was a long, hard process that required self-denial and work.

Second, it requires us to look outward. To be consumed with shyness or indifference may have emotional roots or it may be merely being consumed with self. Disciples of Jesus must focus their attention outward in servanthood. We do not listen to others or serve others because we happen to feel like it; we do it out of obedience. I usually find that my compassionate feelings follow obedience (if they were not there at the beginning).

Finally, learning to care for others requires sound theology. Nothing should warm our hearts more than remembering what Jesus is like. We cannot love him long without loving what he loves. We must not forget that Jesus was an agent of creation. His image, however marred now, is stamped in each one of us. That means that whomever we touch bears his image.

Mother Teresa, an Albanian nun who set up a "Home for the Dying" in Calcutta, India, discussed this point in a talk she gave at the Forty-First International Eucharistic Congress in Philadelphia.[1] She said that after mass one morning she spoke to a group of sisters. "During the mass," she said, "you saw that the priest touched the body of Christ with great love and tenderness. When you touch the poor today, you too will be touching the body of Christ. Give them that same love and tenderness."

Several hours later a young nun came to her, her face radiant. "I have been touching the body of Christ for three hours," she said. Mother Teresa asked her what she meant. "Just as we arrived, the sister brought in a man covered with maggots. He had been picked up from a drain. I have been taking care of him, I have been touching Christ. I knew it was him," she said.

"That young sister understood what Jesus meant when he said, 'I was sick and you comforted me,' " Mother Teresa comments. "Jesus comes to us as the sick and the homeless, he comes to us in the distressing disguise of the poor."

While we might hesitate to endorse all that Mother Teresa says, we are reminded here of Jesus' own comment to his disciples as he took a child into his arms: "Whoever receives this child in my name receives me, and whoever receives me receives him who sent me" (Lk. 9:48). This is a radical statement. It necessitates that we treat human life as sacred and precious, not to be manipulated on the basis of our whims or desires. It reflects what we noted above, that there is something of God's image in every person. Furthermore, when God became flesh in Jesus Christ, he showed graphically the value and dignity of all human life. No matter how distressing the disguise, Jesus tells us that when we receive one such as this we have received him.

C. S. Lewis made the same point when he wrote:

It is a serious thing to live in a society of possible gods and goddesses, to remember that the dullest and most uninteresting person you talk to may one day be a creature which if you saw it now, you would be strongly tempted to worship or else a horror and a corruption such as you now meet, if at all, only in a nightmare.... There are no *ordinary* people. You have never met a mere mortal.... But it is immortals whom we joke with, work with, marry, snub, and exploit—immortal horrors or everlasting splendours.... Next to the Blessed Sacrament itself, your neighbor is the holiest object presented to your senses.[2]

We must see in our neighbors their inherent worth and dignity. In an article in *Campus Life* a young nurse writes of her pilgrimage in learning to see in a patient the image of God beneath a very "distressing disguise."[3]

Eileen was one of her first patients, a person who was totally helpless. "A cerebral aneurysm (broken blood vessels in the brain) had left her with no conscious control over her body," the nurse writes. As near as the doctors could tell Eileen was totally unconscious, unable to feel pain and unaware of anything going on around her. It was the job of the hospital staff to turn her every hour to prevent bed sores and to feed her twice a day "what looked like a thin mush through a stomach tube." Caring for her was a thankless task. "When it's this bad," an older student nurse told her, "you have to detach yourself emotionally from the whole situation. Otherwise you'd throw up every time you walked into her room." As a result, more and more she came to be treated as a thing, a vegetable, and the hospital jokes about her room—room 415 —were gross and dehumanizing.

But the young student nurse decided that she could not treat this person like the others had treated her. She talked to Eileen, sang to her, encouraged her and even brought her little gifts. One day when things were especially difficult and it would have been easy for the young nurse to take out her frustrations on the patient, she was especially kind. It was Thanksgiving Day and the nurse said to the patient, "I was in a cruddy mood this morning, Eileen, because it was supposed to be my day off. But now that I'm here, I'm glad. I wouldn't have wanted to miss seeing you on Thanksgiving. Do you know this is Thanksgiving?"

Just then the telephone rang, and as the nurse turned to answer it, she looked quickly back at the patient. Suddenly, she writes, Eileen was *looking at me . . . crying*. Big damp circles stained her pillow, and she was shaking all over."

That was the only human emotion that Eileen ever showed any of them, but it was enough to change the whole attitude of the hospital staff toward her. Not long afterward, Eileen died. The young nurse closes her story, saying, "I keep thinking about her. . . . It occurred to me that I owe her an awful lot. Except for Eileen, I might never have known what it's like to give myself to someone who can't give back."

What struck me about this nurse and about the young nun is that they knew the poor in their midst. I wonder how many

of us really know the poor? Mother Teresa asks the hard
questions:

> Do we know the poor in our own family? Maybe the mem-
> bers of our family [or church, or college fellowship] are not
> hungry for a piece of bread, maybe they're not naked or
> homeless, but do any of them feel unwanted or unloved?
> ... The Missionaries of Charity care for the crippled and
> the unwanted, the dying and the hungry, the lepers and the
> alcoholics. But the poor come to all of us in many forms.
> Let us be sure that we never turn our backs on them, wher-
> ever we may find them. For when we turn our backs on the
> poor, we turn them on Jesus Christ.[4]

Practicing the Presence
of Christ

8

I WAS WALKING THROUGH O'Hare Airport in Chicago recently when my purse slipped and everything tumbled out. As I was stuffing things back inside, a young woman with a baby stopped to ask the time. Then she nervously bit her lip and asked, "You don't know where I could get a drink, do you?"

I didn't. But as I searched her face, I saw that she was distraught. So I stood up and initiated a conversation.

She quickly interrupted with, "Do you know how much a drink would cost here?"

I could see that we were getting nowhere, and suddenly I heard myself saying, "Gee, I don't know, but would you like me to go with you to find the bar?"

"Oh, would you? I would really love the company," she responded.

Off we went. And all the way I was kicking myself for it—going to a bar at noon with a perfect stranger. How unorthodox! Then I thought, "I wonder what Jesus would do in a situation like this?"

That is just the point. What would Jesus do? In the previous chapter we saw the power and the perspective that Christ's presence brings into our lives. But what is our responsibility in being good stewards of the gift of Christ's presence? In this chapter we will look at four ways we can practice the presence of Christ: seeing people as Jesus does, loving them as they are, loving them as we are, and being salt and light in the world.

Seeing People as Jesus Sees Them

Often we are blind. We act as if those around us were not really people like us. If we see them bleed, we pretend they aren't really hurting. If we see them alone, we tell ourselves that they like it that way.

But Jesus wants to heal our sight. He wants us to see that the neighbor next door or the people sitting next to us on a plane or in a classroom are not interruptions to our schedule. They are there by divine appointment. Jesus wants us to see their needs, their loneliness, their longings, and he wants to give us the courage to reach out to them. If we are to do that we need to do two things: we will have to take risks as well as get beneath the surface of people's lives.

To take initiative opens us up to the risk of rejection. To let people inside our lives is a frightening but essential ingredient in evangelism. It is risky to abandon our security blankets in order to penetrate the lives of others. At O'Hare I wondered what I should do now that I was in the bar with the nervous woman I had just met. I realized that Jesus would probably be more concerned about why she needed a drink than about going into a tavern. I knew that if I couldn't be at ease around her when she had a drink in her hand and allow God to lead me into what he perceived as a mission field, then I wouldn't be very effective in communicating God's unconditional love.

After we found the bar it took only minutes before she began sharing that she had decided to leave her husband. Her husband, unaware of her decision, would be meeting her at the airport in Michigan. She was petrified at facing his response and felt totally alone. "Oh, but it's ridiculous telling this to a complete stranger. How boring this must be for you!" she would comment and then talk on.

The saddest part was her obvious inability to believe anyone could care for her. She trusted almost no one. When she mentioned a problem with which I told her I could identify, she said, "Oh, so that's why you act as if you care. Listen, aren't you afraid of picking up strangers like me? You really should be more careful."

As I began to tell her who God was and that he was the one who brought me into situations like this, she seemed to hang on every word. Soon we were walking to her plane, but I felt torn. I wanted to reach out to her and tell her how moved I was by her problems and that God cared deeply for her. But she was so cold and defensive that I feared her rejection. Finally at the gate I took her hand and said, "Listen, I want you to know that I really care about you, and I'll be praying for you the minute you get off the plane."

She just stared blankly. Then, turning away, she said, "Um . . . I'm sorry—I just don't know how to handle love," and walked away.

The encounter wasn't a smashing success, but I felt I had been obedient. Being a Christian means taking risks: risking that our love will be rejected, misunderstood or even ignored. Now I'm not suggesting that you race to your local bar for Jesus. But if you find yourself in a situation in which you believe God has put you, then accept the risk for his sake.

Seeing beneath the Crust
Second, we need to see beneath the crust. We must never assume that a person will not be open to Christianity. Again

and again I have had to learn that the least likely looking people have been the most open to God.

Several years ago I was on a bus sitting next to a woman in her late sixties. Her face was hard, she was chain-smoking, she wore thick pancake make-up, and her eyes were vacant. I initiated a conversation but her responses were blunt and cold, so I quickly stopped and began working on a talk I was preparing. I thought I would have plenty of time to do paper-work because she was so spiritually closed.

A few minutes later to my surprise, she said, "What in the world are you doing? You look very busy. What are you writing?"

I tried to avoid answering her question directly because I was certain she would not understand. But she said, "Sure it's a nice day. But what are you doing?"

I gulped, told her what I did for a living and that I was preparing a talk for a Christian fellowship.

"You work for God, huh?" she answered cynically.

I knew that was a dead end, so I said, "Tell me your name. And what do you do?"

She said, "I'm Betty. Listen, I'm really busy too, just like you. I've got lots of friends. I just never have a moment to myself. Of course I . . . ah . . . well I live alone. But I have so many hobbies that I never seem to notice." Her answer was sadly revealing.

"You know, I've never lived alone. I guess I'm kind of afraid I'd get lonely," I said.

Suddenly she spun around in her seat and looked at me with great intensity. "Look, girl. You talk about lonely? I'm so lonely I want to die. Half the time I feel I already have. What I said about having lots of friends? Yeah, well I don't. Nobody cares. My heart is bad, and when I feel funny I run outside, 'cause if I die, at least somebody would know. You talk about God. I'm gonna tell you something. I came here to see a guy. I think he kinda liked me. He was lonely like me and we just got on. I called his apartment and he didn't answer. So I called the landlord and asked him if Jack was there. He told me to hold on. When he came back on the line he said, 'Oh, Jack is here. But he's dead. Looks like he died a few days ago. That's a shame. I'll take care of it. Goodbye.' Is that what'll happen to me? I just lie dead on a floor for two days and nobody knows? What's your God say about that?"

As pitiful as Betty's face was, it was the most alive I had seen her during the whole conversation. Pain had forced her out of her deadness and defenses. She hurt too much to be complacent; she had to be real. It seemed as if she were coming up one more time for air.

I mumbled something like, "Makes you wonder if there really is a God, doesn't it? Makes you wonder where in the world Jack is now."

She answered, "I keep asking those questions. But I got no answer. Been asking those questions over and over since it happened."

"When did you learn that Jack had died, Betty?" I asked.

"Last night. And I been up all night . . . just askin' the silence for an answer," she said.

I wanted to weep. Not only for her tragedy, but for my blindness and for the goodness of God toward me. I had sat next to a woman whom I dismissed on sight as being unopen spiritually. But she had been up all night asking ultimate questions. I had wanted to ignore her so I could write my talk on "evangelism." But she was asking questions from her depths, and God was reaching out to her.

I told her that I had never known pain as she had. But I knew others who had known the grief of loneliness. I told her of someone who felt God made sense out of her brokenness. Betty looked hopeful for a few seconds, then wistfully said, "You are so young, so young."

The conversation moved on to other things. I tried to think of some way to reveal God's love. It was clear that for Betty words were cheap. Later in the conversation I said, "Listen, I get to Salem fairly regularly. What if I visit you when I come?"

It was the second time she brightened. Her eyes lit up and she said, "You don't mean it? Sure you could come! Listen, I'm a great cook too! And you could meet my dog. We'd have a great time!"

But when we arrived in Salem, she had become tough again. As we got off the bus and she opened the door to the bus station, she said, "Well, kid. It's been okay meetin' you. See ya around." And she walked off. Then as she approached the other side of the station she stopped, turned around, and looking at me in desperation said, "Oh, God, Becky. Don't forget to call. Oh, please, don't forget me." And she left.

I sat down in the terminal and wept.

I wish there was a happy ending to Betty's story, but there isn't. I visited her. I spent nights with Betty and her dog. I brought students over to meet her, and they loved her far more consistently and faithfully than I. To my knowledge Betty only took. She never gave. Perhaps she was unable to. In fact she used us. She was so starved for love that she could only gulp it down and grab for more. She came to know about the source of our love. She knew about Jesus. But she never chose to follow him, at least while we knew her. I met her and I left her a woman alone.

Betty was not a waste of our time. She was important to God and important to us. We did not fail God with Betty. But we cannot make anyone become a Christian. We are not judged by our success, but by our faithfulness and obedience, though it was a costly and painful obedience for us.

We must never assume that people are as they appear. All of us have needs. Like Betty most of us have experienced some form of rejection. We long for things we are scared to death to ask for. We long to be touched, to be appreciated, to be told we are special, but we do not know how to ask. When we have been hurt, we have tender areas, like open sores that make us deeply fear being touched and exposed. Still, that is what we long for most of all. What we need is for someone to act like Jesus, to put arms around us, to reach out to us and say, "Come home with me. I care about you. I want to be with you."

And that is also what we are called to do. We must not wait until we are healed first, loved first, and then reach out. We must serve no matter how little we have our act together. It may well be that one of the first steps toward our own healing will come when we reach out to someone else. When we get beneath the surface of a person we will usually discover a sea of needs. We must learn how to interpret those needs correctly, as Jesus did. Jesus wasn't turned off by needs —even needs wrongly met—because they revealed something about the person.

The Samaritan woman had had five husbands and was currently living with a sixth man. The disciples took one look at her and felt, "That woman? Become a Christian? No way, why just look at her lifestyle!" But Jesus looked at her and came to the opposite conclusion. What Jesus saw in her frantic male-hopping wasn't just looseness. It wasn't her human need for tenderness that alarmed him, but rather how she sought to meet that need. Even more, Jesus saw that her need indicated hunger for God. He seemed to be saying to the disciples, "Look at what potential she has for God. See how hard she's trying to find the right thing in all the wrong places."

That blows the lid right off evangelism for me. How many Samaritan men and women do you know? Everywhere I am, I see people frantically looking for the right things in all the wrong places. The tragedy is that so often my initial response is to withdraw and assume they will never become Christians. We must ask ourselves, "How do I interpret the needs and lifestyles of my friends? Do I look at their drinking or sleeping around and say, 'That's wrong' and walk away?

Or do I penetrate their mask and discover why they do this in the first place? And then do I try to love them where they are?"

I was talking with a person who had a promiscuous lifestyle. He said cynically, "Bet you're going to tell me it's sinful, huh? Well, I could care less."

I said, "That's probably true. You could care less about yourself and God couldn't possibly care more. You know why God hates sin so much? Because it's the opposite of who he is. It's destructive and can only lead to brokenness. God weeps at what you're doing to yourself because he wants your best— your wholeness."

We can show people that they are right to want to fill the void, and then they may be surprised by joy to discover that the emptiness inside is a God-shaped vacuum.

Loving People Where They Are

In order to establish trust with people we must love them with the baggage they bring with them. We need to accept them where they are without compromising our Christian standards. Jesus accepted the "gift" from the prostitute at Simon's banquet (Lk. 7:36-50). He shattered his "testimony" by allowing a loose woman to touch him. But he did not ask her to demonstrate her love for him and sense of forgiveness by exegeting Ezekiel. He allowed her to offer a gift that she was comfortable with.

We too must live with the tension of being called to identify with others without being identical to them. That may mean that we demonstrate our support by affirming a friend's motive even if we cannot participate in the deed.

A girl moved below me in my apartment building in Portland, Oregon. Every time I saw her she was on her way to another party. We always exchanged friendly words and one day she said, "Becky, I like you. You're all right. Let's get together next week and smoke a joint, okay?"

I replied, "Gee, thanks! I really like you too, and I'd love to spend time with you. Actually I can't stand the stuff, but I'd sure love to do something else."

Of course she looked a bit surprised, not so much because I didn't smoke grass, but because I had expressed delight at the thought of spending time with her. I could have told her, "I'm a Christian and I never touch the stuff," but I wanted to affirm whatever I possibly could without selling short Christian standards. Too often we broadcast what we "don't do" when we should be trying to discover genuine points of contact. Most of us tend either to overidentify and blend in so well that no one can tell we are Christians or to separate ourselves and play it safe by having little contact with the world. We should recognize what our tendency is and work against it.

There are, of course, some things that we should not do. One test is whether the activity violates a scriptural principle. Another is whether we are violating our own sense of purity. Here it is important to know ourselves.

We must be aware where we are vulnerable. Under most circumstances it is dangerous to talk ourselves into what we know is a real temptation but say we prayed God would give us strength to overcome. Often students tell me they entered perilous situations because they felt they were the only person who could witness. I believe we must take risks as Christians. But God will not call us into situations he knows we cannot handle. He can find someone else to go who does not struggle in that area.

Loving Others as We Are

Our message is not that we have it all together. Our message is that we know the One who does! That means we have the freedom to fail. It also means we have the freedom to be ourselves—plus.

Let God make you fully you. Rejoice in your God-given

temperament and use it for God's purposes. God made some of us shy, others outgoing. We should praise him for that. But if you are shy, remember that your shyness is not an excuse to avoid relationships; rather it means you will love the world in a different way than an extrovert.

A girl told me once that she was dreadfully shy. Just the thought of talking to someone terrified her. But she was a committed Christian and knew she had to find ways to reach out. She was perceptive and realized she shouldn't ask God suddenly to make her a boisterous extrovert. Rather she asked him for the freedom to look outward, not to look at herself and be paralyzed by fear. She told me she got a summer job as a waitress because it would force her to talk with people.

When she returned to the university, she applied some newly learned lessons. When she was eating in the cafeteria, she would ask her table, "I'm going back for milk. Can I get anyone anything?" Usually a few would reply yes. When she returned with what they requested, it almost immediately opened up conversation and they asked her questions. She said the fact that they were both focusing on the extra milk she had in her hand reduced her fear of eye-to-eye contact. Her being able to focus on something else (even if it was a piece of pie!) kept her from focusing on herself. That led her on to discovering other ways to serve.

She had a plant that everyone admired. So when someone said she had a beautiful plant, she would say, "Thanks! Let me give you a cutting." That offer opened conversation but kept her focusing initially on the plant, which helped her fears. She also offered to help students preparing for tests if they were in her field or needed a paper typed. Eventually after much practice and continually raising the stakes, she became more and more at ease around people. It was a learned skill. But what freed her and helped her to love and accept herself— and others—was learning that she could take initiative and that people responded to her. She was still reserved but not so desperately afraid. She loved people powerfully but quietly.

What struck me about her was the effectiveness of her non-verbal witness. She told her friends about Jesus. But she demonstrated him in beautiful ways too. She worked on over-coming her timidity, but discovered eventually she had the gift of serenity. People were drawn to her because her presence brought a sense of peace. She would have never realized this gift if she had not gone through the excruciating process of taking initiative. She worked on the "limits" of being shy, but in the process God blossomed in her the gifts of her shyness.

It is dismaying to hear people say that it is easy for me to evangelize because I am outgoing. Being an extrovert isn't essential to evangelism—obedience and love are. There are many people I could never reach, and would probably only intimidate, because I am outgoing. God will have to use other Christians to reach them. But I don't feel guilty about it be-cause God isn't glorified in my life if I try to wear my best friend's personality. I must be who I was created to be. And I must reach out to others in a way that is both sensitive to the person with whom I am talking and consistent with my own personality.

But regardless of our temperaments, we all must become initiators. The mark of a mature Christian is whether she or he chooses to be the "host" or the "guest" in relationships where being a host is most appropriate. There are, of course, times when those who are ordinarily hosts should be guests. The point is that the call to love those around us is in part a call to identify their needs. Once we have some understanding of their needs, we must find ways to meet them that are natural for us.

"But," you may say, the fact is that to "take initiative in itself is not natural for me. I'm just a shy person." Actually, the ability to get outside of one's own skin and serve another is not natural for anyone. But sitting back and doing nothing is not an option. We are called to love, to serve, to identify need and to respond. That is not easy for anyone, but it is what the Holy Spirit helps us to do so we can become more like Jesus. Nonetheless, in the way we exercise our love, the way we choose to demonstrate it, the way we share Christ with others we can choose a style comfortable for us.

The Christian must be the one who loves, cares and listens first. We all can take initiative, whether quietly or openly.

Being Salt and Light

We must not become, as John Stott puts it, "a rabbit-hole Christian"—the kind who pops his head out of a hole, leaves his Christian roommate in the morning and scurries to class, only to frantically search for a Christian to sit by (an odd way to approach a mission field). Thus he proceeds from class to class. When dinner comes, he sits with the Christians in his dorm at one huge table and thinks, "What a witness!" From there he goes to his all-Christian Bible study, and he might even catch a prayer meeting where the Christians pray for the nonbelievers on his floor. (But what luck that he was able to live on the only floor with seventeen Christians!) Then at night he scurries back to his Christian roommate. Safe! He made it through the day and his only contacts with the world were those mad, brave dashes to and from Christian activities.

What an insidious reversal of the biblical command to be salt and light to the world. The rabbit-hole Christian remains insulated and isolated from the world when he is commanded to penetrate it. How can we be the salt of the earth if we never get out of the saltshaker?

Christians, however, aren't the only ones to blame. Even the world encourages our isolationism. Have you ever wondered why everyone always "behaves" when the minister comes to visit on a television program? Suddenly their language changes and their behavior improves. Why? They want to do their part to keep the Reverend feeling holy. They will play the religious game while he is around because he needs to be protected from that cold, real world out there.

Sometimes non-Christians will act oddly around us because they are genuinely convicted by the Holy Spirit in us, and that's good. But all too often they are behaving "differently" because they feel that is the way they are supposed to act around religious types.

I am often put in a religious box when people discover what my profession is. Because I travel a great deal, I have a clergy card which sometimes enables me to travel at reduced rates. The only problem is that occasionally ticket agents won't believe I am authorized to use it! A young female just isn't what they have in mind when they see a clergy card. More than once I've been asked, "Okay, honey, now where did you rip this off?"

Once when I was flying from San Francisco to Portland I arrived at the counter and was greeted by an exceedingly friendly male ticket agent.

"Well, hel-lo-o-o there!" he said.

"Ah . . . I'd like to pick up my ticket to Portland, please."

"Gee, I'm sorry. You won't be able to fly there tonight."

"Why? Is the flight canceled?"

"No, it's because you're going out with me tonight."

"What?"

"Listen, I know this great restaurant with a hot band. You'll never regret it."

"Oh, I'm sorry, I really must get to Portland. Do you have my ticket?"

"Aw, what's the rush? I'll pick you up at eight. . . .'

"Look, I really must go to Portland," I said.

"Well, okay. Too bad though. Hey, I can't find your ticket." He paused, then said, "Looks like it's a date then!"

"Oh, I forgot to tell you, it's a . . . special ticket," I said.

"Oh, is it youth fare?"

"No, um, well, it's . . . ah, *clergy*," I whispered, leaning over the counter.

He froze. "What did you say?"

"It's clergy."

"CLERGY!?!" he shouted, as the entire airport looked our way. His face went absolutely pale, as he was horrified by only one thought, "Oh, no. I flirted with a nun!"

When he disappeared behind the counter, I could hear him whisper to the other ticket agent a few feet away, "Hey George, get a load of that girl up there. She's *clergy*." Suddenly another man rose from behind the counter, smiled and nodded and disappeared again. I never have felt so religious in my entire life. As I stood there trying to look as secular as possible, my ticket agent reappeared and stood back several feet behind the desk. Looking shaken and sounding like a tape recording he said, "Good afternoon. We certainly hope there have been no inconveniences. And on behalf of Hughes Airwest, we'd like to wish you a very safe and pleasant flight . . . Sister Manley."

As humorous as this incident was, I think it shows how difficult it is to maintain our authenticity before the world. The challenge is to not allow ourselves to become more or less than human.

We know, in short, that Christ desires to have a radicalizing impact upon us and our relationships. But that impact is greatly aided when we live as we are called to live: no longer regarding anyone from a human point of view but desiring to see beneath the crust, to love people as they are with the gifts they have to bring and to care in ways that correspond to who we are as well. We are not insulated and isolated from the world but neither are we complacent and blind to its agonies and sorrows and the darkness of its heart. We are salt and light. We make a difference because we are different. And when we live before God as we truly are, he will change the world in which we live.

Developing Conversational Style

9

A PROFESSOR AND I WERE HAVING a stimulating conversation on a plane when he asked what I did for a living. When I told him I worked with Inter-Varsity Christian Fellowship, he looked at me quizzically as if he were thinking, "Funny, and she *looked* so intelligent too."

It was clear he was trying desperately to select the right words to say to a missionary type. In a stilted way he finally said, "I'm sure it must be ... ah ... very rewarding."

"Well," I said, "I'm not sure it's as rewarding as it is intriguing."

Almost in spite of himself he said, "How do you mean, intriguing?"

"I think one of the hardest issues a Christian must face is how in the world we know that what we believe is true. How do we know we are not deluding ourselves and worshiping merely on the basis of need rather than truth? Or that Freud is not correct in saying we worship a glorified version of our father-figure. To have to deal honestly with those questions is exciting and intriguing."

He looked at me in surprise and said, "You won't believe this but those are the very questions I have. Well, how do you know it's true?" For the rest of our flight we discussed the evidences for the Christian faith.

This is one kind of conversational skill. It involves being the first to suggest the defenses that a non-Christian may have. Walls are torn down and bridges are built when we suggest their own objections. In this chapter we will look at ways of moving conversations from discussion of ordinary topics to spiritual ones. We will examine a variety of ways of communicating our faith.

The way we communicate is as important as what we communicate. In fact the two cannot really be separated. Our attitude and style communicate content just as do our words.

If we notice that non-Christians seem embarrassed, apologetic and defensive, it is probably because they are picking up *our* attitude. If we assume they will be absolutely fascinated to discover the true nature of Christianity, they probably will. If we project enthusiasm not defensiveness, and if we carefully listen instead of sounding like a recording of "Answers to Questions You Didn't Happen to Ask," non-Christians probably will become intrigued. Learn to delight in all their questions—especially the ones you can't answer. I often tell people I'm very grateful that God is using them to sharpen me intellectually when I am stumped by a question. I tell them I don't know the answer but can't wait to investigate it. And usually I do investigate and learn in the process.

Just today, as I write this, I had lunch with a student interning in Washington, D.C. She told me her officemate was close to accepting Christ but needed Christian friends.

When she introduced me to her, she said to me, "Well, this is the one." Then she looked at her officemate and said, "Now I'm having Becky meet you because you really need friends.

You'll never make it with God unless someone sticks close to you. So I want Becky just to look at you. Then if she meets somebody, she can send them over to care for you. We've just got to find you a friend."

I wanted to crawl under her desk. But as I tried to think of some cover, the officemate looked at me, smiled and said, "You know, she really, really loves me. And it always shows."

Although love covers a multitude of conversational sins, there are some principles that will help us be better communicators of our faith.

Exposing and Imposing

First, we can learn to expose our faith, not impose it. We cannot make someone a Christian. Consequently we must remember to let our faith be known but not feel we are called on to foist it off on others. In fact, if our evangelism reflects an aggressive style, it could indicate our misunderstanding of the role of the Holy Spirit. We cannot convert anyone if our life depended upon it. Only the Holy Spirit does that.

I used to worry constantly after witnessing to someone whether I did it right, if I should have said this or that, and so on. The Scripture calls us to excellence, but it also says the Spirit will give us what we need for tough situations (Mk. 13:11). To be anxious about whether we have witnessed in exactly the "right way" implies there is some outside perfect standard that we are being judged by. But there is no magic formula; there is no absolute and correct way to witness every time. We are called to do the very best we can, and then trust the Holy Spirit to speak to a person through what we say and do.

Taking It Easy

Second, we need to relax. Since it is the Holy Spirit's job to convert, that should help to ease our anxiety. Again, I am not saying we should be sloppy or lack diligence. But we will probably be more effective with an initial casual reference to God than nervously wondering about our timing.

A student, wringing his hands and looking distraught, said to me, "I have a roommate. And I want to witness to him. But I keep wondering when the right time is. I mean, *when* should I *do it* to him? At what moment must I really tell him? How will I know when the exact time is to finally do it?" By the time he had finished his question, he had me feeling as uptight and intense as he was. And I could not help but sympathize with whomever the recipient of this talk would be. That kind of anxiety would scare a person to death!

It is far more winsome to toss out a few casual comments about your relationship to God or about your Bible study. There is something very appealing about openness. Say, "Hey, I'd like you to meet a friend who's in this fantastic Bible study I'm in," or even, "We had an interesting study this week on how Jesus related to women. He sure was ahead of the culture of his day in his attitude toward women." And then see what happens.

We should talk the same way to non-Christians as we do to Christians. In most instances we should be able to tell both groups the same stories or experiences or thoughts. This will help us avoid having an us-and-them mentality. We should not assume that our non-Christian friends will not be interested in our spiritual side. We need to invite them into our lives, to share what we share, enjoy what we enjoy. We must not act superior because we know God or have more information. Rather, we must be, as someone has said, "one beggar sharing with another beggar where to find bread."

Getting Rid of God-Talk

Third, when we explain the Christian message, we should learn to do so in plain language—hopefully in fresh and creative ways. Few things turn off people faster or alienate them more easily than God-talk. Without realizing it we use words or clichés that have a correct understanding only among Christians. At an evangelistic dorm talk a non-Christian student asked me, "What does it mean to be a Christian?"

A Christian student who really desired the other student to understand replied, "It means you have to be washed in the blood of the Lamb." The first student paled and looked confused. The Christian continued, "That way you will be sanctified and redeemed."

Another student seeking to help his Christian brother said, "And the fellowship is so neat. Praise the Lord! You really get into the Word and get such a blessing." By the end of the conversation one would have thought these Christians came from another planet.

To the world, evangelical clichés are often either red flags or else the meaning is imprecise. Of course we must not dispense with biblical words and concepts. Instead we need to develop fresh and relevant ways to express what they mean. Frequently I will describe what a word means, then say, "That's what the Bible means when it talks about sin." If we do it in that sequence we can arouse curiosity and diffuse defenses.

For example, I was walking out of an English class one day after the professor had discussed the question, "Is the human dilemma tragic?" A fellow student and I began talking about what he had said.

"You know, the Bible says the human situation is tragic. . . ."

"Oh, I know," she interrupted. "You Christians say we are all sinners."

"But Joan," I responded, "do you know why? The Bible says it's because something very, very precious has been broken. If we weren't so significant, if we didn't have so much meaning, then it wouldn't be so sad. It's only when something precious has been broken that we can say, 'How tragic!' That brokenness is what the Bible calls sin. That's why God hates it so much. It caused something extremely precious to become dehumanized."

Here are other common Christian terms we should learn to express in fresh ways: *grace, salvation, justification, sanctification, regeneration, redemption, born again*. And the following phrases also need our creative touch: *having a personal relationship with Jesus, asking Jesus to come into your heart, feeling Jesus in your heart, getting a blessing, getting into the Word*. Your Christian group may well have other obscure phrases meaningful to only the initiated. Learn to translate them.

Asking Leading Questions
Fourth, we can learn to ask good questions. Too often we allow ourselves to be put on the defensive. The dynamics are greatly changed when we turn the tables and begin to direct the conversation by asking questions. I remember a skeptical student who said, "I could never be a Christian. My commitment to scholarship makes any consideration of Christianity impossible. It's irrational and the evidence supporting it is totally insufficient."

I answered, "I'm so glad you care so much about truth and that you really want evidence to support your beliefs. You say the evidence for Christianity is terribly insufficient. What was your conclusion after carefully investigating the primary biblical documents?"

"Ahh, well, you mean the Bible?" he asked.

"Of course," I said. "The New Testament accounts of Jesus, for example. Where did you find them lacking?"

"Oh, well, look, I remember mother reading me those stories when I was ten," he replied.

"Hmm, but what was your conclusion?" I continued and as a result discovered he had never investigated the Scriptures critically as an adult. This is all too often the case. But we can arouse curiosity in others to investigate the claims of the gospel when we help them see that their information and understanding about Christianity is lacking.

Another person who was quite hostile to what she perceived

was Christianity told me in anger, "I can't stand those hypocrites who go to church every Sunday. They make me sick."

"Yes," I responded, "isn't it amazing how far they are from true Christianity? When you think of how vast the difference is between the real thing and what they do, it's like worlds apart. Ever since I've discovered what Christianity is really about, the more mystified I am."

"Ah, the real thing? Well, what do you mean by that?" she asked. We talked for an hour about faith because her hostility had been changed into curiosity. God has made us curious. So learn to ask questions.

Helping People See Holes in Their Own System
Fifth, as we talk with people, we can stimulate interest in the gospel by helping them see that their own current view of life has weaknesses. That is, we can help them see the holes in their system.

The basis of this approach is the recognition that everyone has a world view—a conceptual framework in which they place people and events. We can capitalize on this because surprisingly few people recognize their own world view or can articulate why they know their beliefs are true. Mostly their thinking is a smattering of ideas from a favorite professor, a large residue from family background, a bit of opinion from *Time* magazine or *TV Guide*, a few memories from dorm bull sessions and so on. Our job is to help people develop their point of view more clearly, to recognize their beliefs and then push them to the point of conviction.

When we help people clarify their ideas, they will often be surprised to find out how unsupported they are by any hard evidence or how haphazard and inconsistent they now appear even to themselves. It is at this point that we can help people push their ideas to their logical conclusions and help them see why their positions are inadequate. That does not mean they will be led to conversion. On the contrary, a lot of people are

content having conflicting beliefs floating around in their
head. But for some people, the realization that their beliefs
are inconsistent or inadequate will make a difference.

We need to raise questions that deal with the source of
authority. In other words, we ask why they believe what they
do. Is something true for them because it subjectively "feels"
right or because of a tradition they were taught or because
they believe it is scientifically sound?

For example, a person may be at the point of questioning
the goodness of human nature. He used to be a humanist and
optimistic; now he is not so sure that we are essentially good
and that with a bit more education we will establish a "brave
new world." We need to start where he is, explore his ideas
about human nature, raise questions and suggest alternatives
(that is, the Christian view about these various issues). Maybe
that is all the further we are supposed to go in the first conversation or several conversations. But we have accomplished
a great deal if we have been able to help him see, for example,
that we as people can create beauty, appreciate love, respond
heroically at times, yet that we are deeply in crisis, that we
struggle with greed and selfishness, and hurt those we love,
and that all the education and technology we have acquired
cannot seem to curb this. Maybe we will be able to tell him
God's solution to this dilemma in the first talk, or perhaps it
will come later. But we must deal with each person's actual
questions. And if they do not have any questions with their
present position, we need to raise some for them.

Tom, a student at Willamette University, was talking with
his non-Christian friend about human nature. Tom asked,
"Well, what do you think is the biggest problem in the world
today?"

His friend answered, "Universal greed and selfishness."

"So what is the solution?" Tom asked.

"More education," the student answered.

Now at that point Tom could have said, "No, you idiot

Everyone knows education will not root out evil. The only one who can do that is Jesus!" But Tom was astute. He knew he had to bring his friend to the point of realizing that his idea was faulty. So Tom said, "You say *all* people, *everywhere,* are selfish? And the solution is education? Well, if all people are selfish, then who is going to teach the class?"

The fellow student looked at him, smiled and said, "Right on. It won't work. But we must stamp out selfishness. How? You got any ideas?"

Tom then told him about Jesus, and he was ready to listen because Tom not only had listened to him but had helped him see the flaws in his own understanding.

We will return to the themes in this section when we discuss philosophic evidences. Here it is sufficient to point out that we must discover where people are and take them seriously. Ask them questions about their position and help them see the holes. Then they may be ready to hear what the Christian perspective is. We may be led to communicate only one aspect of the gospel, or we may be led to share much more of it. That will depend upon the receptivity of the non-Christian and our sensitivity to the Holy Spirit.

These five principles of conversation are applicable to most of our dialog with non-Christians. They can be applied any time and any place. As we shall see in the following chapter there are specific models that can help us, too. But what we have learned here applies to any of them.

Three Conversational Models

10

ALL ALONG WE HAVE BEEN TALKING about evangelism as a lifestyle. We have looked at Jesus' life and examined a few practical conversational skills so that we may become more natural and at ease in sharing our faith. I do not now intend to change my basic approach. Techniques can be helpful to some people in limited ways, but they will not make us natural. So what follows here is not a new, never-before-revealed technique of lifestyle evangelism.

Still, what I am about to say may sound like technique or make you feel stilted. If so, then ignore it. I merely want to offer three models that may help you get started. These are not three slick steps to successful soul winning, nor will they move every conversation inevitably to things of God. They are simply three possible patterns we might well be conscious of as we talk to people.

We all have different temperaments. Some of us are cognitive, others of us intuitive. Some respond naturally to ideas illustrated through graphs or charts, others are repelled by them. That is what makes communication with any person exciting and at the same time complex. So when examining any technique or model, we need to ask ourselves, Does this correspond to the way I relate to people? Or does it seem artificial and feel awkward? And even if it feels comfortable for me, would it be appropriate for the person to whom I am speaking?

It is important to realize we are at least halfway responsible for how a conversation goes. We have choices in how we communicate. We should want to make our conversation count in representing Jesus Christ. But that brings us back to Jesus' own example. Jesus directed his conversations, for instance with the woman at the well. He did not manipulate her, yet he did not allow red herrings to get him off the track. He was not molded by her presuppositions; her alternatives did not keep Jesus from his.

So, to have purpose and ultimate desires for a conversation is not wrong. And it is not wrong to learn a few principles of communication to help us get a conversation going as well as to direct it toward spiritual matters. Here are three models that some have found helpful in moving conversations from ordinary topics to spiritual ones.

Model A: Investigate, Stimulate, Relate

Investigate. First we must discover who the person is. This requires a genuine interest and curiosity in that person. Our culture does not encourage us to ask each other questions. We can fly from Los Angeles to New York and never speak to the passenger next to us. But Christians are not to be molded by their culture. We must learn to ask questions, draw people out, so that it becomes part of our lifestyle and not a technique.

In order to do that we need to learn how to be listeners first and proclaimers second. It is like rowing around an island, carefully viewing the shoreline for an appropriate mooring —a shared interest or a shared problem. Look for ways that God has made you alike. The more interests you have, the easier and quicker those mooring points are discovered. For the sake of Jesus Christ we need to be interesting! The more we enjoy God's world and develop our gifts, as well as explain new interests, the easier it will be to establish rapport with others.

If we listen for the nuances, we can draw others out without prying. Many people hesitate giving direct messages because they are not sure anyone really wants to listen or are afraid that they cannot be trusted. Frequently people give clues about what things are bothering them or where they feel need. For instance, in response to "How are you?" someone says, "After last week things could only go up." Or as in the case of Betty when she said, "I live alone, but I have so many hobbies that I never seem to notice," which was an even more hidden message.

Sometimes people give us direct data but do not elaborate. For example, a person once said to me, "Thanks for the invitation but I can't. I went to a funeral last week and now I'm bogged down with homework." In both cases the ball has fallen into our court. We must find a way to express concern and give them an opportunity to talk *if they want to*. We must approach with care any "message" that we think we hear. If we sense need, it is probably because they intended for us to hear it. Sometimes you may hear a need and feel you are not the person to meet it. Then find a person who can.

Even if you are suddenly tongue-tied and walk away feeling you blew it, it is not too late. Go back later and say, "Listen, I'm so sorry about your grandfather's death. I just couldn't think of what to say to you the other day. But I care, and I'm praying for you" (be sure you do actually pray). That may open just as many doors as an initial statement of condolence.

Stimulate. After we have an idea of whom we are talking to,

we must seek to arouse their curiosity about the gospel. This is
one of the most neglected aspects of evangelism. We try to
saturate people with the light before we have caught their
attention. In Acts 26:18 Paul says Jesus first called him to
open the eyes of others before helping them turn from darkness to light. He was called to arouse their interest so they
would want to hear his message. This is part of being "fishers
of men" rather than "hunters of men." A look at Jesus and
Paul to study their fishing techniques will be helpful.

Jesus was often deliberately vague and intriguing with
people at first, not giving the whole answer until he had their
complete interest. He knew that the Samaritan woman (Jn. 4:
7-42) wouldn't understand what "living water" meant any
more than Nicodemus (Jn. 3:1-21) would comprehend the
term "born again." Here deliberate obscurity was a stimulus
and test of their spiritual interest.

Paul aroused the curiosity of the Thessalonian Jews in the
synagogue with his fierce logic and rational arguments (Acts
17:1-8). In Athens he captured the interest of the Greeks by
citing their poets to affirm his points (Acts 17:28).

We too need to develop a style of intriguing evangelism.
How can we pique interest in the gospel?

Relate. When we have discovered where people are and have
aroused their interest in what we have to say, we are ready to
relate the gospel message. Investigating and stimulating are
the necessary pre-evangelistic steps that will enable us to communicate Christ more effectively. But it is not enough to take
the first two steps without the third. Paul, for example, knew
his audience, found where they needed to grapple with commitment and then proclaimed the gospel (Acts 17:16-34).

Notice that Paul's message to the Athenians contained content and not just experience. Somehow it is difficult to imagine Paul on top of Areopagus defending his faith before secular philosophers by saying, "Gee, I dunno, fellas, it's just this
feeling in my heart." Our conversion experience may illus-

trate the power of the gospel, but it does not explain it. I cringe sometimes at the lack of content I hear when students are sharing their faith. Jesus begins to sound more like a happy pill to be popped, a trip to beat all trips, than a Lord to be obeyed at any cost.

We need to have a basic understanding of the Christian message, so when we do feel led to give it we can. There are lots of tools that give the Christian message. One of them breaks it into four parts:

1. The nature of God: his purpose
2. Human nature: our dilemma
3. Jesus Christ: our solution
4. What we do: our response

Inter-Varsity has a card called "First Steps to God" (see appendix I) that uses this outline. God is the natural place to begin. He is the Creator, the source of all that exists. But he is not just an amorphous power that brought the universe into being and set it in motion. He is a person who is actively involved in all that he has created. He is a person who loves us perfectly (Jn. 3:16). He is also a God of total justice, punishing evil, expelling it from his presence (Rom. 1:18-32).

How do we human beings relate to God? First, because he has created everything, we are his creatures. We were originally made for his own purpose—to be in fellowship with him, to obey him, to relate to him person-to-person (Col. 1:16). But we rejected this offer; we rejected his purpose, his rule (Is. 53:6). As a race we have rebelled against God. As individuals we have turned away. The result has been separation, loss of fellowship with God (Is. 59:2). Because God is just and holy, because he cannot accept anything that is evil, he hands down the penalty of eternal death (Rom. 6:23).

But because God is also love, he simultaneously seeks a way of reconciliation (Col. 1:19-20). That was why Jesus came as a man—to die, to pay the penalty for our sins that we deserved, to actually take on our sins in his body (Rom. 5:8), and then to rise to new life, making eternal fellowship possible for us (1 Cor. 15:3-4; Jn. 10:10). His gift is eternal life (Rom. 6:23).

God will not, however, force his love on us. He will not require us to have a reconciled relationship with him if that is not our choice. To complete reconciliation with him, we must each admit that we have rebelled (Mt. 4:17), confess that we cannot be reconciled to God apart from what Christ did on the cross (Jn. 1:12) and accept Christ's purpose, rule and power in our lives. Through prayer we can invite him to live in us (Rev. 3:20).

Such an outline of the gospel is one option. John Stott's booklet *Becoming a Christian* is another. There are many others. Find one that you are comfortable with and that is biblical, not sidestepping the problem of sin, the need for repentance or the call to yield to Christ as Lord.

After you find or devise a tool that accurately summarizes the Christian message, then make it your own. Write out in your own words how you would express the fundamentals of the faith to a friend. We need to have an answer to someone who says, "What is a Christian and how do I become one?"

As a younger Christian I felt wobbly in my ability to explain what I believed. So I carried around booklets that expressed far more articulately than I could what I believed. I have listed several helpful booklets in appendix II. Once a girl told me she wanted to become a Christian but did not know how. So I took out a booklet and read her the essence of the gospel and asked her if she believed it. When she said yes, I told her I would pray with her.

I do not need the support of a booklet now, but it was valuable then. But we must remember that God does not ask us to give a polished, slick presentation of the gospel after day one. He asks us to be faithful in sharing what we know and what we have seen.

We will look later at how to help a person enter into a new relationship with God in Christ. Before we do that, however we need to consider other ways to move conversations from common interests to spiritual matters.

Model B: Concentric Circles

The concentric circles model I owe to Donald C. Smith who developed this while he was a staff member for Inter-Varsity Christian Fellowship in Michigan. Conversations, he says, can be like an onion. As we peel off the layers in a conversation, we go even deeper into the mindset of a person. Often conversations begin with general interest questions (What is your major? What do you do for a living? Where is your home?) Then we ask more specific questions (What era of history are you specializing in? What do you enjoy about your job?). We frequently miss the next layer, but it is crucial; this is the abstract or philosophical layer (Why are you majoring in history? How does your art reflect the nature of humanity? Are you satisfied with what psychology is teaching you about people?). And then the theological layer (What do you think God demands of us?).

Here is what the model looks like:

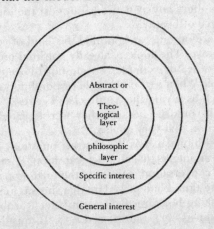

Here's how the model works out in practice. For example, I was talking to a student and asked: "What is your major?" (general interest question).

"Art," Peggy answered.

"I really think that's a great field of study. Why do you major in it?" (specific interest question).

"Well, I guess because I appreciate beauty," she said.

"I do too. You know I had a biology professor who said we are nothing more than meaningless pieces of protoplasm. Do you think a piece of protoplasm can appreciate beauty?" (abstract or philosophic question).

"Mmmm, I've never thought of it before. But we must be more than that. The appreciation of beauty runs so deep in us," she said.

"One thing has always intrigued me. Where do you suppose beauty comes from? I mean, what's its source? And where do we get our ability to appreciate beauty?"(theological questions).

"You mean like God or something? I don't know but it's interesting to think about."

"Well, is there any evidence to support the idea that God is the source of beauty?"

From here on one can continue this kind of conversation in many ways. The topic is already spiritual and it can be natural to raise, for example, the question of beautiful people —like Jesus. When we hear people responding to their God-image (such as saying they appreciate beauty), we can help them see it could be because they were created by a God who enshrines that very quality.

The transitional key is the abstract question. It does not have to be an intellectual abstract transition. For example, in my earlier conversation with Betty the turning point was the abstract question. I had picked up that she was lonely. But instead of asking her directly about it (which probably would have frightened her), I abstracted it to "It must be lonely to live alone." She responded by opening up her whole lonely life to me.

It could be that this model is not one you will find helpful. Fine. Perhaps you will find the following model more consistent with your style.

Model C: Relationships, Beliefs, Epistemology

Mark Petterson provides a third model for how to develop conversations with non-Christians. He says, "In any conversation the content is controlled to a large extent by the questions. If you want to control what is discussed, then you must take the initiative in asking questions."[1] He then defines three areas that conversations (and consequently questions) deal with: relationships, beliefs and epistemology.

Relationships: how a person stands with respect to a common denominator (school, major, number of children, etc.). This is like the "investigate" part in Model A and the "general interest question" in Model B. Conversation in this area is relatively easy and relaxed. We can usually find something of mutual interest.

Beliefs: everyone has beliefs about politics, love, the meaning of life, God and so on. You might ask, "What do you think about—Carter, abortion, women's lib, the 'born again' movement?" It is in this area of beliefs that conversation can break down. Meaningful interaction cannot take place at this level if the beliefs are not shared. Conversations can soon degenerate into argument, each person solidly maintaining their previously conceived dogma and not listening or interacting with the other. For example, someone may say, "I think this 'born again' thing is for the birds. It's just a new fad."

You instantly say, "No! It's not. It's a legitimate experience."

The other person is convinced to the contrary, the battle lines are drawn and fruitful interaction is ended.

How can we avoid the impasse and move into dialog? The key is to move the conversation to the third area.

Epistemology: ask, "*Why* do you think this 'born again' experience is not legitimate?" This allows the conversation to continue and very often forces people to admit that what they believe about many important things is mere personal opinion. Asking why makes people disclose their authority.

It may be possible, then, for the Christian to move the discussion on and show how Jesus provides authoritative information. If Christ's claim to be the living God is true, "then his answers to the meaningful questions of life are of the utmost importance," Petterson writes.[2] By asking epistemological questions the Christian can often make any meaningful conversation naturally focus on Jesus Christ, who is the central issue.

It is also in this area that Christians must know not only who their authority is, but *why* he is reliable. That probably means being able to cite some evidence for the historicity of the gospel. We will take up the use of evidence in our conversations in chapter eleven.

The Final Step
The goal of evangelism is to bring people to Christ so that he can bring them to new life. If we are following the leading of the Holy Spirit and living like Jesus, as we talk with people, we will come to the place where they may ask, "Okay. I would like to be a Christian. How do I do it?"

There is probably no experience more terrifying than the first time we lead a person to Christ. But there are few things more thrilling or that make us more aware of how true Christianity is. To see God's Spirit take control and beautifully change a person's life is one of the greatest miracles we will ever witness. So we must be willing to help people enter into a relationship with God if they are ready.

When people tell us they want to become Christians, we need to be sure they understand and believe the essence of the

gospel: including the nature of God as just and merciful, the
nature of human beings as sinful and separated from God, the
nature of salvation through the death of Christ, the necessity
of repentance and acceptance of Jesus as Lord as well as
Savior.

If all these things are clear, then I believe we need to suggest
reasons why they should *not* be Christians. Becoming a
Christian involves turning one's entire life over to Christ's
control. As we have seen with both Lois and Cathy in chapter
three, God expects us to live holy lives, being generous with
our time, our money and our active compassion for people.

People also need to know before they decide what they will
have to do to stay spiritually alive. Daily Bible reading and
prayer are essential, as is belonging to a Christian community.
Young Christians need to find a church that is vital and alive,
and they should meet with a small group of Christians regularly for Bible study, prayer and fellowship. We can help them
for the first few weeks until they are more secure. It takes a
long time to learn to live in God's world in God's way, so we
need to be there to help them begin. And we must bring
others along to help them too.

If they still want to give their lives to God, we can ask them
to pray and ask Jesus to be their living Lord, confessing the sin
of running their own lives and asking him to take charge.
Then we can pray with them confirming his work in our life
and thanking him for entering theirs. John Stott suggests that
those who wish to take this final step echo the following prayer
in their heart:

Lord Jesus Christ, I acknowledge that I have gone my own
way. I have sinned in thought, word and deed. I am sorry
for my sins. I turn from them in repentance.

I believe that you died for me, bearing my sins in your
own body. I thank you for your great love.

Now I open the door. Come in, Lord Jesus. Come in as
my Saviour, and cleanse me. Come in as my Lord, and take

control of me. And I will serve as you give me strength, all
my life.
Amen.[3]

Born Again in Barcelona

Leading someone to Christ is an experience all of us should
have. It confirms the truthfulness of the gospel and the reality
of God's presence as few other things do. In case you feel
inadequate, let me tell you about my first experience.

After my failure with Mary in Barcelona I asked God to
help me be more brave the next time around. Ruth Siemens
kept telling me that when the time was right I should ask my
friends if there was any reason they could not become Christians right now. The Bible study was nearing an end for that
year, and all of us were studying for finals. After one exam
Todd and I went for a cup of coffee in a student restaurant.

Of all of the students in the study, he was the most cynical to
the gospel. He made Mary in her agnostic days look like
Mother Teresa. Initially he came only to disrupt the study, but
we befriended him and eventually he came every week. There
was only one more study left and I felt I had to ask somebody
in that group to become a Christian. I was sure Todd would
never become a Christian. (I really did not think I would be
instrumental in anyone's conversion till I was at least eighty!)
So Todd seemed safe.

So I said, "Todd, you've been in this study all semester.
You've heard a lot about God, but you've never decided what
to do with God. One of these days, Todd, you're going to have
to decide. Sooner or later God is going to speak to you and say,
'Decide now.' And what are you going to say?" I was feeling so
proud for sounding firm (even though I knew my confidence
stemmed only from the fact that he would never respond) that
I failed to notice how serious his face became. "Yes, sooner or
later, Todd, God is really going to speak to you. And when he
does, in that year, I hope you will say yes."

I think I was still speaking when Todd said, "You're right. God is speaking and I am saying yes."

But I went right along without inhaling, "That's right, Todd. One of these days God will reach out—ah, wh-what did you just say?"

"I said, 'God has been speaking to me right now. And I said yes,' " he answered.

I paled. "Oh Todd," I answered weakly, "you have such a sense of humor. But really, you shouldn't scare me like that."

"Becky, I'm not kidding. I've been thinking about this for a long time. And I'm ready now," he replied.

"Todd, listen to me. You can't rush into this. I mean it's a huge decision. And it'll change your life so much. You better think it over and then go see Ruth."

"Look, Becky. This isn't an emotional decision. I know I put up a good front, but I've been thinking about God for a long time. Now look, I want to become a Christian!" he nearly shouted.

"Right here? In the restaurant? In front of everybody? Todd, I just, well, I can't."

"Why not?!"

"Well, because I've never done anything like this before."

"Don't worry, I haven't either," he answered. "I tell you what. Let's close our eyes. Then I'll say something to God and then you do. It'll be over in just a few minutes."

So we did, right there in a restaurant in Barcelona, Spain. When I opened my eyes, I still thought it was only temporary. But even if his conversion only lasted a few hours, it would have been enough for me. I said, "Now Todd, something Ruth always says is that conversion is a matter of your will. It doesn't matter if you don't feel any different," since I was sure he didn't. "It's your will that you've given to God. The emotions will come later. But there is just one thing I wanted to ask you," I said.

"Sure, what is it?" he asked.

"Ah, do you feel any different," I asked.

"You bet I do!" he roared.

I looked at him in utter shock. "Todd!" I cried, "it works!" So off we went to my apartment to tell Ruth and Kathy.

While we were there, Stephanie, another agnostic friend in the Bible study, called and asked us to do something that night. During the evening I kept thinking how flabbergasted she would be when Todd told her, especially since he was one of her best friends. We were in a restaurant when she looked at Todd and said, "You know, you've really changed. You just look happier, more peaceful. Spain must really agree with you."

And Todd responded, "It isn't Spain, Stevie, it's God. I've become a Christian."

She, thinking he was joking, said, "Yeah, right. I'm Santa Claus. You shouldn't joke like that in front of Becky."

"Stevie, I'm serious. I've given my life to Christ. I intend to follow him."

She looked incredulous but then terribly anxious. He was the least likely of all of them to turn to God. If Todd could, then what did that mean about the others? She grew quiet and serious as Todd told us of his spiritual pilgrimage, that he always had hid behind his sarcasm and seeming indifference. We took a cab home. Stephanie decided to stay over with me. We walked into my room and she said, "I want to know how he did it. What do you do when you become a Christian?"

Now I could have lived off Todd's experience for a good twenty years. But when I saw how seriously she asked me that question I thought, "Oh, it couldn't be! It couldn't happen again. I just can't handle this."

So I said, "Stevie, would you excuse me for a few minutes?" I casually walked out and shut the door. Then I panicked. It was 1:30 in the morning and I needed help. Kathy and Ruth were asleep, but I went into Kathy's room anyway. I burst open the door and couldn't think of anything to say. So I yelled, "Pray!" and wheeled back out. Kathy told me she awoke with such a start that she prayed for ten minutes before realizing she did not know what she was praying for! Back in my room Stephanie and I talked quietly for several minutes.

Then she said, "Becky, I've been running away from God for a long time. It's time I start running to him," and she became a Christian that night.

As reluctant and inept as I was, that night changed my life. Before my eyes I saw the very two who seemed the least likely turn their lives over to Christ. Perhaps even as significant as that experience eight years ago is that today Stephanie is a mature Christian who married a Christian man. I am the godmother of their child. God is faithful. And little did I realize that a feeble attempt to witness to one girl would produce a family who loves God.

There are people around us whom God longs to touch through us—people that only we can reach with our particular style and personality, people whom we have been called to. We must begin to ask God, "Is this the one? Is she the one you are seeking?" It is a fantastic drama, and God wants to use us to accomplish it.

Giving Reasons for Our Faith

11

LET'S SAY RALPH NADER HAD A conversion experience. Now for Nader facts are everything. But what if he suddenly declared to the public, "I had this incredible experience last week while looking at my tulip patch. I'm now a believer. And I get up early every morning and bow down and worship the tulip seeds"?

I bet many people would say, "Oh, wow, that's really beautiful, Ralph. You know, whatever turns you on is okay. I mean as long as it works for you then that's great." Only a few would say, "How do you know it's true? How do you know you're not creating your own little world and calling it 'reality'?" We would check his facts in any other area but this one, because in religion, we are told, as long as we are sincere then it is true enough.

But something is wrong here. Hitler was sincere, drug addicts are sincere, the followers of the People's Temple in Jonestown were sincere. Sincerity just cannot be an adequate

basis for determining truth. Our concept of truth in religion
has been so drastically reduced that something is true if it
makes us feel good or comes from sincere motives. But as the
adage goes, we need more than sincerity because we can be so
sincerely wrong!

What we need is a faith that corresponds to the reality
around us, that makes sense out of our world, that is internally
consistent and hangs together. As Christians we do not have
absolute proof for our belief in Jesus. There is in fact no absolute proof for any ultimate proposition, whether Christian
or Buddhist or atheist or whatever. But the God of the Bible
does not call us to leap in the dark; he does not require faith
without evidence, for that is mere superstition.

I used to feel frustrated as an agnostic asking Christians
truth questions when they always answered, "It's just this feeling in my heart."

"But I need something for my head too!" I would respond.
And to my delight I found God offered both. He gives us the
subjective experience of knowing him and objective evidence
to act upon. It is not evidence that overwhelms us or answers
every question, but it is evidence that is sufficient.

To further sharpen the effectiveness of our conversations,
we can learn to employ some basic apologetic skills. In the
process this will build our own confidence in the truth of
Christianity. I will mention briefly three areas of evidence:
historical, philosophical and personal.

Historical Evidence
People often respond very sentimentally to my faith. They
say, "I think it's beautiful what your faith does for you. It's
really your thing. I mean it's not my thing, but it's so nice for
you."

To which I say, "But do you think it's true?"

They usually say no, and so I often continue the conversation in one of two ways.

One way is to say, "How can a lie be beautiful? Either I am right or else hopelessly deceived. If I am wrong, then I have stacked my entire life on falsehood. If I'm deceived, then it's ugly, not beautiful."

Another way is to say, "Despite your thoughtfulness in saying my faith is valid for me because it gives me such a warm feeling, all of the tenderest feelings in the world cannot make a man rise from the dead. Either Jesus did or did not, quite apart from my feelings on the subject. And one of the most attested facts in history is that his tomb was empty. The government turned Jerusalem upside down trying to find the corpse. Either Jesus resurrected or there must be an explanation of what happened to his corpse. But neither conclusion depends on my warm glow to make it true. Jesus isn't true just because he makes me feel good."

This moves us into the arena of historical evidences. Questions such as, How do you know the Bible is historically trustworthy? Was Jesus merely a good teacher? How do you know he was resurrected? Did Jesus even exist? Why Christianity and not other religions? These questions all require evidence. A variety of books in this area can give us surer footing (see appendix II). The questions non-Christians ask are remarkably similar. It would be helpful to have index cards with the problem stated at the top—"Evidence for the Resurrection"—and the basic arguments listed below. Paul Little's *Know Why You Believe* is structured around twelve questions non-Christians most frequently ask. That would be a good place to start learning how they may best be answered.

Philosophical Evidence

Some of the philosophical questions that Christians need to know how to answer are, How could a good God allow evil or hell? Are people basically good but simply misinformed and will improve with the proper controls? Are we merely machines, matter-in-motion? How can we talk of absolutes (that something is "good" or "unjust") when everything is relative or merely by chance?

There are many excellent books that deal with these issues in depth (see appendix II). Here I want to suggest some basic guidelines. Being able to put new ideas or old arguments into proper categories can be helpful. Even recognizing that one question requires historical evidence while another requires philosophical is a start. When someone exposes a thought or system you are unfamiliar with, do not get bogged down in a myriad of details. You need not feel intimidated by a system of thought you do not know. It is impossible to read everything. Try to get at the heart of their system, and that will help you (and probably them) categorize it and understand it properly.

Listen carefully and sympathetically as they articulate their beliefs. Get their views on several issues. See if you can get to the core of their beliefs by asking a few basic questions. It is surprising how relatively few basic answers there are to ultimate questions. The details of systems may differ, but most ideas can be put into a few slots. Here are some examples:

1. *The basic nature of the world.* Do people or their arguments begin from the premise that there is no God, that we started from nothing or from matter only? Or if they believe in God, what kind of God is it (personal or impersonal, finite or infinite, involved with human affairs or aloof)?

Discovering whether they begin from a naturalistic premise or a supernatural one will determine a great deal. For example, if they do not believe in God and maintain that the universe is closed, mechanistic and impersonal, it would be impossible for them to believe in biblical miracles. If they do not believe in the supernatural, then it is pointless to keep arguing about something that their system could never accommodate. We should point out to them, however, that it is utterly consistent for us to acknowledge the possibility of miracles because our system allows for the supernatural. So instead of banging away at the possibility of miracles, we might ask that since they deny the existence of God and the existence of absolute truths, are they able to live consistently with such beliefs?

2. *Morality.* Closely related to the question of whether God exists—and if so, what kind of God it is—is the issue of ultimate morality. If a God who is interested in matters of ethics does not exist, then there may be no basis outside ourselves for determining what is right and wrong. I know many students who think in exactly that way, and they claim to be able to live consistently with that notion.

They advocate "free love," for example, because, since there is no absolute standard of morality, sexual ethics is reduced to a question of taste and preference. Nonetheless—and this is the point—those same students are *rigid moralists* in opposing racial prejudice, child brutality, war and so forth. And why are they against such things? "Because they are wrong, categorically and universally!" they retort.

But we cannot have it both ways. We must play by the same rules on different issues. We can legitimately and forcefully challenge them, "If you say there is no such thing as morality in absolute terms, then child abuse is not evil, it just may not happen to be your thing. And if you find you are not able to practice your premises with much consistency, then you need to re-examine your premises." Most people's response to evil is one of horror. When we read of the mass suicides in Jonestown, our immediate response is "That is wrong! It is evil!" or when we hear of abject poverty or senseless torture, we say, "That is unfair, unjust!" Or conversely, when we see a masterpiece, we say, "It is beautiful." In all this we are seeing people responding to the fact that they are made in the image of God—a good God, a God of beauty.

Our feelings of justice, of goodness, of beauty, stem from the God who enshrines these very qualities and who made us like himself. As C. S. Lewis says, to call a line crooked still implies we know what a straight line is. To protest evil,

as the Marxists do, tells us they have a strong sense of what
is right, and they are angry to see it violated. So we must
ask, Where do our feelings of right and wrong, evil and good,
come from? What is the origin of these qualities? Where did
our culture derive these strong beliefs?

Challenging our non-Christian friends on whether they live
consistently by their own self-acknowledged principles is an
effective way of casting doubt on their present beliefs. Francis
Schaeffer has explained much about this in *The God Who Is
There*. So if you are naturally drawn to thinking or find you
need help in straightening out the issues, reading that book is
a good next step. You may find yourself going back again and
again to it and other books like Os Guiness's *In Two Minds*, or
James Sire's *The Universe Next Door* or C. S. Lewis's *Mere
Christianity* and *Miracles*.

The point is that the Christian world view gives solid, intellectually profound answers to the very questions most
people ask when they find their own answers are inadequate.

3. *Human nature*. Some people think a human being is only
a set of chemicals, a piece of protoplasm. That is a valid philosophical position. But we may ask, Can they live that way?

I had a biology professor who stated the first day of class,
"Man is merely a fortuitous concourse of atoms, a meaningless piece of protoplasm in an absurd world." We were taught
that having deep regard for random products of the universe where chance is king was inconsistent. Some time later
he told our class in despair that his thirteen-year-old daughter
had run away to live with an older man. "She will be deeply
wounded. She will scar, and I can't do anything to help. I
must sit back and watch a tragedy," he said grimly.

I raised my hand and said, quietly, that according to his
system protoplasm could not scar.

His answer was devastating. "Touché. I could never regard
my daughter as a set of chemicals, never. I can't take my
beliefs that far. Class dismissed."

Because we are made in the image of God, no matter how hard we try, we can never escape reacting to the world at some point, like God has made us. Sooner or later we will expose our God image. And when that point comes for the people God has given us to know, we must lovingly challenge them to quit escaping reality and live as they were created to be—children of God.

4. *The fundamental problem in the world and how we deal with it.* Everyone from physicists to poets agree that something is wrong with the world. Philosophies, ideologies or explanations of the life process usually place the blame either on external circumstances or on individual decisions and actions. If they see the source as external, then they usually say the system needs changing. For example, an individual is not bad or selfish, he has just developed poor habits: he is a victim of an externally imposed evil. Whether the evil culprit is the capitalistic economic superstructure as Marx suggested or the environment as behavioral determinist B. F. Skinner theorizes, the focus of blame is outward not inward. The other alternative sees the problem as derived from some kind of internal chaos. Christianity says evil has permeated both levels and we must fight evil at both levels. But the *source* of evil is internal (Mk. 7:14-22).

When we meet optimistic humanists who believe people are basically good, we must agree first. One pillar of our understanding of humanity is that God declared his creation *good* (Gen. 1). Our ability to respond with compassion, to be moved by the beauty of a Da Vinci painting or the soaring Austrian Alps stems from the fact that we were created with wondrously good qualities. But we are not naive about the other aspect of our humanness—our sinfulness. The Bible deals utterly realistically with both sides of us. We are not intrinsically cruel, God did not make us evil. But he made us free. And we rebelled. We are not now what we were created to be. By our own decision we became abnormal when we chose not to be in relationship to God (Gen. 3).

So when optimists say that people are basically good but just need a bit more education or the right controls, we must ask them, "How do you account for two world wars? For rampant bigotry that still exists in our age of enlightenment? How do we write off the atrocities of the Hitler era or of the People's Temple in Guyana? How do we explain Watergate adequately?" My husband, who was principal UPI reporter on Watergate, says, "Watergate provided us a refresher course in basic theology; it reminded us of the reality of evil in a relativistic era. Christians above all others should have understood a basic cause of Watergate—the lure of power, to which so many White House aides succumbed—because it was one of the first temptations with which Jesus was confronted. But it also reminded us of the ever-present possibility of redemption and renewal. Lives were changed for good because of Watergate."[1]

We must not be naive about the reality of evil. Nor can we afford to fail putting tough questions to advocates of the human potentials movement. No one should know or understand better the heights to which humans can climb or the depths to which we can succumb than a Christian. Therefore we must force the world to take both human goodness and human evil with the utmost seriousness. And when their analysis of our dilemma is shallow or their solution merely a Band-Aid approach, we must help them see that.

I was sitting next to a beautiful black law student on a bus to Salem, Oregon. We were discussing our heroes when she told me Karl Marx was her hero. When I asked why, she said, "Because of his passionate regard for the oppressed."

"I agree with that concern," I responded, "but what is Marx's view of the universe? For example, I know he holds no belief in God."

"Oh, yes," she replied, "Marx is very intelligent. He sees the universe as godless, and we have meaning only in a corporate sense of class. We are not significant as individuals."

"Yet you admire his regard for the oppressed even though they are ultimately insignificant. It seems strange to value them so highly when they are random products of a universe. Why not manipulate them as you please?" I asked.

"I couldn't do that. I guess if my natural response is to feel people are significant then I need a philosophic system that says the same thing," she astutely observed. "But I believe we are basically good. If we could live in a classless society, we would be free of the things that weigh us down. I really think on the basis of economic determinism we will be saved."

"Do you really believe if we lived in the ideal Marxist society our problem would be voted out?" I asked.

"Absolutely," she said.

I took a deep breath and said, "Listen. I know a guy. He is one of the worst racists I have ever met. If he lived with you for fifty years in your classless society, every time he saw you he'd still think 'nigger.' How can Marx wipe out the ugliness and hatred of a bigot?"

She turned away from me, her eyes glaring, and, looking out the window she said, "Right on. We've been trying to change that for centuries. And all of the rules and laws in the world can't change you. The laws curb behavior, they can force you to treat me justly, but they can't make you love me."

I knew I had struck a raw nerve but I felt I had to. Anyone who has suffered as blacks have in this society must know that an external change does not mean an internal change. I said, "You tell me you know people are significant, and you need a system that says so. Now you're saying that the real evil comes from within us. For external rules or laws can curb but not transform behavior. So you need a system that regards evil as internal and a solution that transforms radically not curbs superficially. Right?"

"Yeah, well it'll take more than a human attempt to change

us that much. But we need it," she said.

"I couldn't agree more. In fact that's the very kind of system I've found," I said.

"Really? Hey, what revolution are you into?"

When I told her I followed Jesus, I think I had better not quote her exact words of response! But after she recovered from her shock she asked me how I knew it was true. For the rest of our trip she asked me to defend Christianity. She listened intently, and when we arrived she said, "I'd like to get together again. And there's something you're not going to believe. When I went home this weekend my younger sister came to see me, too. Then she told me she'd become a Christian. I told her it was anti-intellectual and unsubstantiated. In a furor I packed my bags, walked out saying I never wanted to discuss it again, got on the bus and sat down next to you."

We do indeed worship the Hound of Heaven.

Personal Evidence

Another effective form of evidence is what God has done in our own lives. The world hungers—perhaps without even knowing it—for examples of evidence in people's lives. They want to know if God works. Has he brought you a feeling of self-esteem? Does God make a difference in a marriage and in raising children?

Earl Palmer said once that perhaps the best testimony a Christian couple can give today is a reasonably good marriage. We who are married do not have to pretend we are living as Barbie Dolls on a wedding cake. We have struggles, and dashed expectations too. But if we offer the world a model of a reasonably good marriage, a reasonably good church, a reasonably good college fellowship, it will have radicalizing effects on the world. We need to tell others what prayers we see answered, what things God is doing. We must communicate his aliveness!

Every Christian has a personal story to tell. Each of you who reads this book is unique. God has called you to be a very specific, very special person, and your story, your life is a testimony to God's goodness, his grace, his forgiveness. So share who you are with people. Let them know you have struggles but that Jesus has made a difference.

I have told many stories in this book—some of which have surprised me even more than the others involved. The changes God has wrought in people always amaze me. But he has wrought good works in you too. Don't be afraid to tell people who you are—and who you were before you met Christ.

True, some people only testify to themselves. "Once I was a louse. Now I'm great." God sometimes drops out of the testimony altogether. Or all of their witness is simply personal—what God has done for them. "I know he lives, because he lives within my heart." We must direct people's attention outward to God in Christ loving and reconciling the world to himself by the death of his Son on the cross. But the subjective dimension is equally real and, when balanced by the objective and historical, is a powerful witness to who God really is.

Whether we begin with historical, philosophical or personal evidence, we want to direct attention to Jesus. We want them to examine him and his claims by what they see in our lives and our minds. We need to offer the world models of "head-and-heart" Christianity.

The Witness
of Community

12

WE HAVE TALKED A LOT ABOUT how individuals can look at Jesus and begin to emulate his values and priorities. We have said that it is the Spirit of God who empowers the individual to live the life that Jesus calls us to. But models of head-and-heart evangelism do not spring solely from individual, personal witness.

We were not born to be alone. God created us for relationship. So we have been born first into the human family and then as Christians born again into the family of God. All of us, therefore, are members of some kind of community, our own family, school, friends, fraternity, sorority or other social groups. As John Donne has said, "No man is an island."

Still, we often feel like islands. Our professional commitments frequently lead us not only into geographical isolation but emotional isolation as well. And so loneliness —the very opposite of community, the most crushing of all emotions—descends on us. There is an important reason for this. It is by design and not caprice that we find loneliness crushing. Only in community can we become fully alive, fully human, finding rest and completeness in the context of others. It is not enough for one individual to imitate the ways of God. For God is not alone; he is the Trinity. Therefore, it is the community of God's people who will represent him more fully and completely.

Furthermore it is in community—in seeing ourselves juxtaposed with others—that we learn who we are. In community we can exercise the gifts God has given us. In all likelihood these gifts are gifts of ministry. For Christians especially community is glorious. For it is in community that we can worship together, be nurtured and bear one another's burdens.

What, then, is the role of Christian community in evangelism? Some Christians feel that their community (be it a church, a Bible study, a small group or a friendship relationship) can prepare people to be launched out for witness to others. Certainly we need to be fed and nurtured and built up and trained. But we must remember, too, that our local Christian community itself can be a powerful witness to our non-Christian friends. Communities of Christians who practice what they preach arouse and stimulate curiosity in Jesus. When the teaching of Jesus is heard and demonstrated, there will be impact.

No Lone Rangers

We are not called to be "Lone-Ranger" Christians. We are called to love one another. Indeed a legitimate basis for rejection of belief in God, according to Jesus is lack of love among Christians (Jn. 17:20-24). The antihero for Christians is the American cowboy, out there dodging the arrows and bullets alone. Instead we are called to be a close family that welcomes the world into our midst. We invite people to come and share our love and our gifts. We are free to admit we have not arrived and are far from perfect. But because we believe Jesus is the living center of our group, we invite our non-Christian friends and acquaintances to hang around us and observe him.

I used to feel paranoid about the presence of skeptics in Christian groups. Would they feel weird listening to us pray? Watching us read the Bible? When I gave a talk to a group, I used to ask the leaders if there were any nonbelievers present. Upon reflection I realized that even if there were, I would not change my message at all. The world is not as fragile as we think. They can handle us in our natural habitat far more than we realize. All they need is to feel welcome and to be invited to "come and see." In fact, people long to be a part of a community who will care for them (whether it is a Bible study group or a church).

Although that truth is ageless, it has never been more timely than today. For a variety of reasons, people are drawn in more often by the warmth of relationship than the brilliance of apologetics. In fact, people are almost too vulnerable to community; if they feel loved, they will tend to believe anything. This situation is exploited to the fullest by a number of the fringe religious groups like the Unification Church of Sun Myung Moon. As Christians true to Christ we do care about emotional needs, but we must be careful not to manipulate people through it. It is fine that the world is drawn into our midst because they feel welcomed and cared for. But we must be as concerned for their minds as for their souls. We must offer not only love but excellent biblical teaching as well. There has to be solid intellectual content in our warm communities or our houses will be built on shifting sand. The world needs both to feel God's love and hear God's truth in us.

Communities, then, can be powerful tools to communicate the reality of Jesus. Let us take a closer look at some of the forms these communities take.

Christian Bible Study

Our witness as a community can be especially demonstrated through a Bible study group. The group should think of activities to which they could invite their friends. Bruce Erickson, an Inter-Varsity staff member in Oregon, said that his Bible study learned of a man on welfare whose house needed reroofing. Bruce suggested that each member bring a non-Christian friend and make it a "roofing party." Someone would have to be pretty desperate to go to a party like this. But a group spent the day together, working hard, caring for the man and just having fun.

Some of them eventually became Christians. Without realizing it these Christians had been witnessing all day by the way they cared for each other, by their concern for the man, by their ability to have fun! We need to invite people along to see us as we live. Things we take for granted (that we pray for each other, sincerely try to love each other) can make a deep impression.

Another way we can make a lasting impression on the world is in our attitude toward possessions. Jesus talks about few things as much as our possessions. He tells us that no person can serve two masters (Mt. 6:24). To serve God as our first love means there can be no competing loyalties. We can stimulate a curiosity in the gospel when we demonstrate that we believe our money is God's and we desire to use it to please him.

One of the things that grabbed Lois's interest in the gospel was when she came to a fellowship meeting and heard a Christian student say he had no money for a ticket home. Immediately three fellow Christians reached into their pockets and gave him what they had. Later when Lois wanted to go to a Christian student conference but had no funds, another Christian told her he would sell his camping tent. He loved camping but he felt that her getting nurture for her young faith was more important. When we demonstrate a biblical attitude toward money and material possessions, the world stands up to take notice.

Or take another example. Once a girl told me her Bible study group wanted to reach out to their non-Christian friends, but they could not think of what to do. Then she said quickly that she had to dash to pick up tickets for her group to see *Richard III,* a play she was in. When I told her that would be a great thing for them to take their friends to, she said, "What does *Richard III* have to do with God?"

"For starters, this play deals with the problem of evil. Is Richard responsible for his cruelty or can he blame it on his 'genes' and his crippled body? Any discussion of the nature of evil leads one to discussing ultimate issues," I said.

So here we have an example not only of what to do, but also of the importance of integrating our faith into our world. If we think God is relevant only in Bible studies, our witness will have little impact.

That means we need to be conscious of current political and cultural events. It is not necessary to see or read everything, but we do need to be aware of what our culture is listening to. Then we must develop our analytical skills in evaluating our culture from a Christian perspective. We need a "Christian mind," as Harry Blamires has suggested. I know a woman who does not go to many films. But she reads Pauline Kael's film reviews in the *New Yorker* regularly to gain understanding and awareness of her culture, and it helps her to talk with others. Unfortunately her example is the exception.

When through our Bible studies we reach out to our skeptic friends in love and bring them into our midst, when we live as Jesus would have us live, regarding people as infinitely more important than material things, and when we demonstrate sensitivity and insight rather than ignorance toward our culture, the impact will be great. Our Christian group, then, will not become ingrown and isolated from the surrounding society. Rather we will demonstrate that Christians are real

people who care deeply for other people. We study and love
the Scripture because it, too, is passionately honest about life
and loyal to the truth about us. We meet together as Christians, and we pray and study God's Word because we celebrate
the call to live in the real world and are not trying to escape
from it.

Nonetheless, perhaps we feel bringing our non-Christian
friends to a Bible study full of Christians would be too over-
powering at first. We may feel they need something less
threatening to start with.

Evangelistic Bible Study

Sooner or later we must get our non-Christian friends reading the Bible. One effective way is to gather several skeptic
friends with one or two Christians and study a passage that
vitally confronts us with the person of Christ. They need to see
Jesus as he walks through Palestine—watch what he does, listen to what he says, observe how he relates to people. This was
how his disciples slowly became convinced of who Jesus was.
Our friends, too, need to hang around the Jesus in the Gospels.

Many people blindly accept Christ's deity as a child, and
then blindly reject it as they grow up, without ever realizing
that Jesus comes to us first as a person. Our aim is to allow
Jesus to come alive to them in the Scriptures to give them a
feel of what kind of person he is.

When you invite your friends, assure them that no previous
Bible knowledge is necessary. They do not have to believe in
God or the Bible. The point is for them to read firsthand
what the Bible actually says. If they do not believe, then for
the sake of intellectual integrity they need to know what they
are rejecting. We can assure them that it will not be churchy;
we will not sing hymns. Rather we will study the passage as we
would any historical document, arriving at conclusions that
the text, not the teacher, demands.

This is an efficient way to present Jesus. Most people do not recognize their need for Jesus in a one-shot conversation. But when a Christian befriends them and eventually leads them into a study like this, they will grasp a much fuller picture of what it means to be a Christian. Even if we only met six times, we could look at: (1) Jesus' sensitivity and compassion to people (Jn. 4: the woman at the well); (2) his miraculous powers (Jn. 11: Lazarus's resurrection); (3) who he claimed to be (Jn. 14: "I am the way, and the truth, and the life"); (4) how to become a Christian (Jn. 3:1-21: Nicodemus); (5) the death of Jesus (Jn. 19); (6) his resurrection (Jn. 20).

Most importantly, to lead this kind of study it is not necessary to have lots of experience or training as a Bible study leader. The leader needs to draw out the members as to what the text says, not lecture for an hour.

If you would appreciate help in knowing how to ask the right questions and draw people out, it is not hard to find. Ada Lum has written a very brief but handy guide called *How to Lead an Evangelistic Bible Study* to give sound general help. And she has put together a series of studies on the life of Jesus called *Jesus the Life Changer* which selects key events in the gospels and suggests specific questions you can ask. I have mentioned other such tools in appendix II.

The Church

I have said very little about the local church because most of my experience has been within a parachurch organization. It is not that I feel the church is unimportant. On the contrary, all Christians should be involved in a church. Parachurch organizations are not the norm. They will come and go, but the church, the agent of God's action in the world, is for the ages.

Moreover, the church can offer to the world a model that a college Christian group never can. It can offer the model of unity amidst great diversity—diversity of age, race, occupa-

tion, ability, interest and so forth. There are inevitable limits
to a model of Christ which includes only people who range
in age from eighteen to twenty-one.

If you are reading this as a student and you are not associated with a local church, let me say, go immediately and find
one where Christ is exalted, the Bible is trusted and acted on,
and begin worshiping there. For only there will you find the
full scope of what Christian community can mean.

The question is, then, how can churches become communities of faith reaching out and offering life to the world
around them? I have often asked pastors how effective their
congregations are in reaching out to their local area. Frequently they tell me that their programs are not effective.
Many have tried a highly stylized method of evangelism but
with meager results. The church members were unaffected,
and so was most of the community.

One pastor told me his church spent hundreds of hours
training members on exactly what to say as they went door to
door sharing the gospel. Three years later, after a tremendous amount of time and effort, only one person who claimed
to become a Christian was still walking with God. He said the
reason was that the Christian who came to his door cultivated
a genuine friendship with him and invited him to meet his net-
work of Christian friends.

The pastor was so struck by that that his congregation
began focusing on building strong small group neighborhood
Bible studies. He provided Bible study and small group
training and encouraged them to reach out to their non-
Christian neighbors. For the first time the members of his
church began to trust each other, love each other and become
truly involved in each other's lives. Then when they formed
friendships with non-Christians in their neighborhood, they
genuinely wanted them to meet their friends in the Bible
study. Soon the Bible study members were bringing their non-
Christian friends to their group and eventually to their

church. The pastor told me that for the first time during his ministry there real evangelism was going on in his church.

There is a reason for this. Using structures like door-to-door knocking or tracts or a prepared speech is not necessarily wrong, but such methods have limits. They may be useful to a person who has never opened his or her mouth about God and who needs something to start the ball rolling. We all have to start somewhere, and if we feel that a certain method helps us initiate a conversation, then so be it. The ultimate aim, of course, is for our evangelism to flow naturally from our lives and thus reflect a style that is truly consistent with who we are. But no one arrives at that destination all at once. It may take lots of practice, false starts and perhaps even mechanical beginnings before we feel at ease in witnessing.

There are, however, limits to using techniques to talk to a person about Christ. Door-to-door knocking may help get a hearing, but once you are inside the door, your orientation can never be the same again. You only meet a stranger once. From that first meeting some kind of relationship will follow.

It is the same with surveys—asking a person a set of questions designed to draw out their interest in spiritual matters. They may be helpful the first time you talk to a person. But you can only use a survey once. The next time you see that person you cannot whip out the same survey or use another opening technique. The closer you become to an individual, the more awkward you will feel using such methods.

Most "contact" evangelism techniques are severely limited by the fact that nonbelievers never see the gospel fleshed out in the believer's life. One of the greatest gifts (and evidence) that we give is the chance to see how Jesus lives his life through us. And the demonstration of his love, his holiness and his charity is far more powerful in a community of believers than in any individual. Strangers, so long as they remain strangers, only hear a message and never see it lived out in human relationships.

Another limit to contact evangelism is that the very style itself is usually associated with salesmanship. Jesus thus appears simply as another product on the religious market.

Moreover, since this is used by so many fringe religious groups, non-Christians often ask, "Now which one are you? Are you into Hare Krishna, the Moonies, Scientology or what?"

We are then reduced to saying, "No, I'm into the Jesus thing." And so we become one option among thousands because our initial approach has been like all the others. We live in a culture of people who feel like burned over ground. They have heard it all. They have been assaulted by every trip imaginable. And when our style or initial approach reminds them of all the others, Jesus is reduced in their estimation to merely one option among many.

I am not saying there is no place for contact evangelism. But I am saying that by far the most effective, the most costly and even perhaps the most biblical kind of evangelism is found in the person or groups who look at the people around them, those with whom their own life naturally intersects and then begin to cultivate friendships and to love them. When churches start to reach out to their neighborhoods through small groups, the impact can be overwhelming.

Freedom to Fail

We can learn a great deal of information, be full of zeal, master conversational skills, walk closely with God, participate in his community on earth and still blow it. That is one reason God told us so many stories of individuals in the Bible. He knew we would need the encouragement!

Take Peter. He loved Christ, and yet he constantly made mistakes. His most grievous error came in the last moments of Jesus' life. Jesus had told Peter he would deny knowing him, but Peter staunchly rejected the idea. After Jesus was arrested, Peter denied three times ever knowing him. He even invoked a curse upon himself if he knew him. As the cock crowed, what Jesus said had come to pass, Peter had denied the Lord.

Imagine how desolate Peter felt after Jesus' death. The last contact Peter had with Jesus was the scene of his own betrayal. In Jesus' most difficult moment when he needed support the most, Peter had turned against him. Then a few days later Peter was told that the Lord has risen. Jesus was alive; his friends had actually seen him.

How did Peter feel now? He probably had ambivalent feelings. On one level he would be ecstatic, but on another afraid and ashamed. Maybe the Lord had given up on him. Maybe Jesus would feel Peter had made one too many mistakes.

But God knew how Peter felt. He had a messenger tell the women who first came to the tomb, "Go tell his disciples and Peter" that he had risen (Mk. 16:7). "And Peter"—two of the most beautiful words in the Bible. So the disciples went and said, "Guess what? Jesus has risen! A messenger from God told us to go and tell you he's here. And, Peter, he said to tell you especially!" Only two words, but they brought a world of hope to a man.

And what did Jesus say to Peter when he saw him (Jn. 21:15-17)? He asked, "Peter, do you love me?"

And Peter said, "Yes, Lord, I do."

And so Jesus asked again, "Peter, do you love me?"

Peter perhaps hesitated a bit, and then said, "Yes, Lord, you know I love you."

And then Jesus asked the third time, reminding Peter only too well of his recent painful history of thrice rejecting Jesus.

"And Peter was grieved" and he said, "Lord, you know everything; you know that I love you."

Peter realized that Jesus knew who he was, his fallibility, his limits, his warts. And yet Peter loved Jesus. Jesus knew that too. He had known Peter's faults long before they ever dawned on Peter. And Jesus told him, "Feed my sheep."

Earlier Jesus had nicknamed Peter (Mt. 16:18). Of all the names to choose, Jesus picked the least likely: he called him Rock. We might have selected another, like Shifty or Quivery or To-and-Fro or Sandy. But Jesus chose Rock.

Jesus is telling us something through this. First of all, he knows us—me, you. He knows your limits, your broken promises, your failures. But he also knows that beneath all of that, you have a heart of love for him. He knows that you care. And Jesus also has a name for you, a name you would have never picked for yourself, or dared to dream. He sees what he is making you into; he knows what he has in store for you. And he gives you a name that suits what you are going to become. We are people of hope and not despair because we have a future that has been secured by God.

More important than our wobbly love for him is his absolute unswerving love for us. When Peter told Jesus he would always remain faithful to him, Jesus knew his resolve would crumble. Nonetheless, he said, "Simon, Simon, behold, Satan demanded to have you, that he might sift you like wheat, but I have prayed for you that your faith may not fail" (Lk. 22:31). And he went on to say, "When you have turned again, strengthen your brethren." Our Lord would not let Peter go. His love is the absolute of the universe.

Jesus knows our warts, but he also knows we love him. He knows what we will look like someday, not a grain of sand as we so often feel, but a beautiful rock, and he loves us, eternally and mightily. And so he turns to us, as he did to Peter, and says, "Feed my sheep." It is that simple. Whatever gifts you have been given, whatever likes or talents, use them, give them, spend yourself on God's world as Jesus spent himself on you. Comfort his people.

Paul prayed as he wrote to the church in Corinth, "Blessed be the God . . of all comfort, who comforts us in all our affliction, so that we may be able to comfort those who are in any affliction, with the comfort with which we ourselves are comforted by God" (2 Cor. 1:3-4). Earl Palmer says that the word *comfort* in this passage is most accurately described like this: a person is walking down a road alone and he is then joined by another who walks alongside so he does not have to walk the rest of the road alone. And so we might retranslate the text this way: "Blessed be the God who has walked alongside of us, who walked alongside of us in óur affliction, so that we may be able to walk alongside of others in their affliction with all of the 'walking-alongsidedness' which we have experienced."

That is what God is like—he is the One who walks alongside. And that is what he calls his children to do. Regardless of age, temperament, fears, inhibitions, he bids us to feed his sheep.

What will we look like? We will look like a man I have only heard about. When I first came to Portland, Oregon, I met a student on one of the campuses where I worked. He was brilliant and looked like he was always pondering the esoteric. His hair was always mussy, and in the entire time I knew him, I never once saw him wear a pair of shoes. Rain, sleet or snow, Bill was always barefoot. While he was attending college he had become a Christian. At this time a well-dressed, middle-class church across the street from the campus wanted to develop more of a ministry to the students. They were not sure how to go about it, but they tried to make them feel welcome. One day Bill decided to worship there. He walked into this church, wearing his blue jeans, tee shirt and of course no shoes. People looked a bit uncomfortable, but no one said anything. So Bill began walking down the aisle looking for a seat. The church was quite crowded that Sunday, so as he got down to the front pew and realized that there were no seats, he just squatted on the carpet—perfectly acceptable behavior at a college fellowship, but perhaps unnerving for a church congregation. The tension in the air became so thick one could slice it.

Suddenly an elderly man began walking down the aisle

toward the boy. Was he going to scold Bill? My friends who saw him approaching said they thought, "You can't blame him. He'd never guess Bill is a Christian. And his world is too distant from Bill's to understand. You can't blame him for what he's going to do."

As the man kept walking slowly down the aisle, the church became utterly silent, all eyes were focused on him, you could not hear anyone breathe. When the man reached Bill, with some difficulty he lowered himself and sat down next to him on the carpet. He and Bill worshiped together on the floor that Sunday. I was told there was not a dry eye in the congregation.

The irony is that probably the only one who failed to see how great the giving had been that Sunday was Bill. But grace is always that way. It gives without the receiver realizing how great the gift really is.

As this man walked alongside of his brother and loved him with all that he had received from Christ's love, so must we. This man was the Good Samaritan. He made Bill feel welcome, feel as if he had a home. So he also knew the secret of the parable of the Prodigal Son: there finally is a homecoming because we really have a home to come to.

Appendix I

First Steps to God

The following is an outline of the Christian message that was developed for students and staff in Inter-Varsity Christian Fellowship. Many have found it a useful summary to keep in mind as they share their faith. You may wish to copy this on the flyleaf of your Bible or xerox this page and tape it on the inside cover. See pages 141-43 for the place of such outlines in evangelism.

God

A. God loves you (John 3:16).
B. God is holy and just. He punishes all evil and expels it from his presence (Romans 1:18).

Man

A. God, who created everything, made us for himself to find our purpose in fellowship with him (Colossians 1:16).
B. But we rebelled and turned away from God (Isaiah 53:6). The result is separation from God (Isaiah 59:2). The penalty is eternal death (Romans 6:23).

Christ

A. God became man in the person of Jesus Christ to restore the broken fellowship (Colossians 1:19-20a). Christ lived a perfect life (1 Peter 2:22).
B. Christ died as a substitute for us by paying the death penalty for our rebellion (Romans 5:8). He arose (1 Corinthians 15:3-4) and is alive today to give us a new life of fellowship with God, now and forever (John 10:10).

Response

A. I must *repent* for my rebellion (Matthew 4:17).
B. I must *believe* Christ died to provide forgiveness and a new life of fellowship with God (John 1:12).
C. I must *receive* Christ as my Savior and Lord with the intent to obey him. I do this in prayer by inviting him into my life (Revelation 3:20).

Cost

A. Cost to God (1 Peter 1:18-19).
B. No cost to you: your salvation (Ephesians 2:8-9).
C. Cost to you: discipleship (Luke 9:23-24).

Appendix II

Books for Evangelism
Published by IVP unless otherwise indicated.

Booklets to be read and given to non-Christian friends

Sir Norman Anderson, *Evidence for the resurrection, The fact of Christ*

Norman Warren, *Journey into life* (Falcon/Kingsway). A graphic presentation of the way of salvation.

John Marsh, *Tree squatters anonymous*. For those who like to look at Jesus from a safe distance! Cartoon illustrations.

Christian Way booklets (small format):

John Stott, *Becoming a Christian, Being a Christian*

Michael Cassidy, *Christianity for the open-minded*. An invitation to doubters

David Gooding, *How? The search for spiritual satisfaction*

Michael Green, *The brink of decision*

Derek Swann, *A faith that is real*

Forum leaflets A series of five leaflets dealing with five basic evangelistic questions.
What does the Bible say?; What is a Christian?; What is sin?; Who is Jesus Christ?; Who wrote the Bible?

Books to be read and given to non-Christian friends

Oliver Barclay, *Reasons for faith*. The author outlines the main reasons for believing that the Christian idea of God is right, and tackles some objections to it.

John Blanchard, *Right with God* (Banner of Truth). No frills or entertainment but a very clear presentation of man's need, the character of God, Christ's work, man's response.

Gordon Bridger, *The man from outside*. This book builds up a portrait of Jesus Christ, seen through the eyes of one who really knew him, John, 'the disciple whom Jesus loved'. New edition, using text of Good News Bible.

Gordon Bridger, *A day that changed the world*. Why did Jesus die? This question which has haunted history is answered clearly and with a minimum of technical language.

F. F. Bruce, *The New Testament documents: are they reliable?* For those with questions about the reliability and accuracy of the New Testament, the author carefully sifts the historical evidence for their reliability.

David Day, *This Jesus . . .* A powerful, sometimes hilarious, look at the average person's reactions to Jesus and how we can find him to be alive and a real part of our lives.

Michael Green, *The day death died*. An examination of the evidence for the resurrection, showing its veracity and challenge today.

Michael Green, *Jesus spells freedom*. A study of Jesus Christ as the only one able to help modern man use his freedom in a proper and reasonable way. Jesus is the free man's model.

Michael Green, *You must be joking* (Hodder). Typical red herrings and other objections to belief. Very readable. Illustrated with cartoons.

Michael Green, *Why bother with Jesus?* (Hodder). Brief chapters on why Jesus is significant – his life, character, death, the effect on us.

Derek James, *Just in time*. An amusing, challenging and unconventional introduction to the Christian faith. Cartoon illustrations.

C. S. Lewis, *Mere Christianity* (Fontana). With clear writing and compelling logic, Lewis brings together insights into the essentials of Christianity. A good general book for the thinking person.

C. S. Lewis, *The problem of pain* (Fontana). The age-old problem of a God of love and a cruel world.

Frank Morison, *Who moved the stone?* (Faber). An exciting look at the events surrounding the resurrection. Here are the results of an investigation of the resurrection by a lawyer who expected negative conclusions but was brought to faith by the facts themselves.

John Stott, *Basic Christianity*. A key book for those who want to examine the evidence for the Christian faith. It sets out to provide answers to such questions as: Who was Jesus Christ? What did he claim for himself? Why was he crucified? What is the evidence for his resurrection? What does it really mean to be a Christian?

David Watson, *Is anyone there?* (Hodder). The difficulties and the reasonableness of belief in God. Cartoon illustrations.

David Watson, *In search of God* (Falcon/Kingsway). Looking for God   man, love, meaninglessness, suffering, and Jesus   God in search of man.

John Young, *The case against Christ* (Falcon/Kingsway). 'Counsel for the defence' in the trial of the reliability of Christianity. It answers the challenges raised by science, suffering, different religions and other common objections.

Evangelistic Bible study guides

Ada Lum and Brede Kristensen, *Jesus: one of us*. A book centred on the Gospels, divided into themes, with notes for leaders and suggestions for discussion.

Gordon Bridger, *The man from outside*. This book builds up a portrait of Jesus Christ, seen through the eyes of one who really knew him, John, 'the disciple whom Jesus loved'. New edition, using text of Good News Bible.

Group Bible study outlines on many topics and individual characters and books of the Bible are available from UCCF, 38 De Montfort Street, Leicester LE1 7GP, England.

More reading on evangelism

Michael Green, *Evangelism now and then*. What were the secrets of the early Christians' impact? Can we rediscover them now?

J. I. Packer, *Evangelism and the sovereignty of God*. A sympathetic examination of the doctrines of the sovereignty of God and human freedom, in the light of the evangelistic task.

Paul Little, *How to give away your faith*. A practical, challenging and enjoyable book on the art of personal evangelism. Cartoon illustrations.

Notes

Chapter 2: Jesus the Evangelist
[1]G. K. Chesterton, *Orthodoxy* (New York: Image, 1959), p. 146.

Chapter 3: Jesus the Lord
[1]John Stott, "Must Christ Be Lord to Be Savior? Yes," *Eternity* (September 1951).
[2]D. Martyn Lloyd-Jones in a talk given to the General Committee of the International Fellowship of Evangelical Students in 1963.
[3]C. S. Lewis, *Mere Christianity* (New York: Macmillan, 1960), pp. 54-55.
[4]Oswald Chambers, *My Utmost for His Highest* (London: Marshall, Morgan and Scott, 1927), p. 265.
[5]Earl Palmer, *Love Has Its Reasons* (Waco: Word Books, 1977).
[6]C. S. Lewis, *Screwtape Letters* (London: Bles, 1942), p. 46.

Chapter 4: A question of Priority
[1]See W. D. Davies, *Paul and Rabbinic Judaism* (Cambridge: University Press, 1948); and E. P. Saunders, *Paul and Palestinian Judaism* (Philadelphia: Fortress, 1977). Saunders is hesitant to say that we know very much about the Pharisees. Our sources are simply too limited. He writes, "It seems quite possible to me that we not only have no Sadducean literature but also virtually no Pharisaic literature, apart from fragments embedded in the Rabbinic material" (p. 426).
[2]Louis Finkelstein, *The Pharisees* (Philadelphia: The Jewish Publication Society of America, 1938), II, 633.
[3]F. F. Bruce, *New Testament History* (Garden City: Doubleday, 1972), p. 73.
[4]Ibid., pp. 73 and 149.
[5]A. T. Robertson, *The Pharisees and Jesus* (London: Duckworth, 1920), p. 44, from the Sanhedrin x, 13.
[6]W. D. Davies, *Introduction to the Pharisees* (Philadelphia: Fortress, 1967).
[7]Finkelstein, I, xxxvii.
[8]C. E. B. Cranfield, *The Gospel according to St. Mark* (Cambridge: University Press, 1959), pp. 236 and 238.
[9]Wesley G. Pippert, *The Spiritual Journey of Jimmy Carter* (New York: MacMillan, 1978), p. 162. This quotation from Niebuhr comes from Jimmy Carter who expanded on it in an address before his Sunday-school class. That a person in such a strong leadership position should enunciate this principle is significant because of his ability to apply it.

Chapter 5: A question of Holiness
[1]Robertson. p. 46, from the Shabbath xxii, 6.
[2]Ibid., p. 44, from the Sotah iv.
[3]Ibid., from the Sopherim xvi, 6.

186

[4]A. Finkel, *The Pharisees and the Teacher of Nazareth* (Leiden/Köln: Brill, 1964), p. 51.

[5]Gustave F. Oehler, *The Theology of the Old Testament* (Grand Rapids: Zondervan, 1883), p. 18.

[6]H. Wheeler Robinson, *The Religious Ideas of The Old Testament* (London: Duckworth, 1913), p. 40.

[7]Wesley G. Pippert, "Holiness: For the Nation and for the Individual," an address given at Forest Grove Reformed Church, Hudsonville, Michigan, June 25, 1978.

[8]Robertson, p. 79.

[9]John R. W. Stott, *Christian Counter-Culture* (Downers Grove: InterVarsity Press, 1978), pp. 24-25.

Chapter 6: A Question of Obedience

[1]Robinson, pp. 73-74.

[2]Jim Wallis, "Conversion: What Does It Mean to Be Saved?" *Sojourner* (May 1978), p. 14.

[3]Chesterton, p. 154.

Chapter 7: Christ with Us

[1]Mother Teresa, "The Poor in Our Midst," *New Covenant Magazine* (January 1977), pp. 15-17.

[2]C. S. Lewis, *The Weight of Glory* (Grand Rapids: Eerdmans, 1949), p. 15.

[3]"Lady in 415," as told to Hope Warwick, *Campus Life* (May 1976), pp. 50-52.

[4]Mother Teresa, p. 17.

Chapter 10: Three Conversational Models

[1]Mark Petterson, "Strategic Conversations," *HIS Guide to Evangelism* (Downers Grove: InterVarsity Press, 1977), p. 45.

[2]Ibid., p. 47.

[3]John R. W. Stott, *Basic Christianity*, 2nd ed. (Downers Grove: InterVarsity Press, 1971), p. 129.

Chapter 11: Giving Reasons for Our Faith

[1]Wesley G. Pippert, address given for the Michigan State University chapter of Inter-Varsity Christian Fellowship, January 23, 1976.